First published in the United Kingdom in October 2017
by Crux Publishing Ltd.

ISBN: 978-1-909979-52-9

CONTENTS

Making It Count: Examinations, Evidence and Outcomes

Making it Happen: Politics, Progress and a Peaceful World

Introduction

This short book represents the concerns, ideas, aspirations – and frustrations – of a group of UK citizens who have been involved in education for a long time. We put it together from start to finish in just twelve weeks - so it represents a snapshot of where we currently find ourselves (although some of the issues discussed within these pages have been around for a long time). We don't claim to represent everyone, but we include authors, former government ministers, classroom teachers, parents, entrepreneurs, CEOs, school governors, university professors and school leaders. We suspect there are many, many more people who feel the same way, but we haven't as yet ascertained how many: our first task was to crystallise those concerns, ideas and aspirations into a vision for change.

Now that we've done that (the vision for change immediately follows), we feel that this is the time to share our ideas, test the waters of public opinion and invite people to join in the conversation.

The common cause that has united us? The conviction that we need to change the conversation around education. For too long, the public debate has been narrow, restrictive and polarised. It's also been overly regressive, often fuelled by the idea of recreating some past golden age of schooling, even as we hurtle into a radically different future. Educational policy-making has become ideological, especially in England – where most of the book's contributors reside. Even something as seemingly objective as the current push for 'evidence-based practice' has become distorted by cherry-picking 'evidence' to suit biases on both sides of the political divide. Media – and particularly social media – only exaggerate these divisions, ensuring false dichotomies flourish in a culture of entrenched beliefs. In short, the conversation has become a shouting match over the heads of our children, who are short-changed accordingly.

Meanwhile, societal and technological change, of a kind never before witnessed, has been hurtling toward us, demanding that we radically rethink every aspect of our lives except, it seems, education reform. It's as though, faced with the sheer scale of problems that our primary-age kids will have to face in the coming years – dominated by automation, artificial intelligence, the impact of climate change and mass economic migration – we've decided to seek comfort in irrelevance. At the time of writing, we have reached the end of the first week of the academic year in the UK. The media is filled with stories of school leaders implementing 'strict discipline' procedures: putting children into isolation because they forgot to bring calculators (they have calculators on their mobile phones of course, but 'no excuses' schools ban their use); sending others home because they wore suede, not leather, shoes. One school, the very week I write this, sent the following 'welcome' to its parents:

> *"... you must support the school 100%. 99% just won't do. At times you may think our approach inflexible, over strict, or unreasonable. But I ask that you trust us...Your children's job is to attend every day on time, follow all instructions first time every time, treat everyone they meet politely, and get the top grades they possibly can in everything they do."*

The school then lists their expectations:

> *"1. Traditional black school shoes in leather or leather look material. Children who do not meet our expectations regarding uniform and appearance will be placed in isolation.*
>
> *2. No mobile phones on the school site. If a phone is seen or heard it will be confiscated.*
>
> *3. Girls may wear one small plain gold stud in each earlobe only. No other piercings. No retainers. If earrings do not conform they will be confiscated.*
>
> *4. No chewing gum on site. If found with chewing gum, pupils will be placed in isolation."*

It's a strange and trivial set of priorities, more redolent of penal institutions than places of aspiration and learning. It must be acknowledged, however, that this hardening of attitudes has partly come about because of the accountability demands now placed upon schools, and because the strains upon teachers, principals and students alike have reached breaking point. The wellbeing of teachers and students in the UK is in crisis: teacher recruitment targets missed five years in a row; almost 50% of teachers struggling with poor mental health; 79% of schools recently reporting an increase in student self-harming and suicidal tendencies. We can't go on like this, and we desperately need some new ideas, but our conversations seem caught in a feedback loop.

We seem fixated upon which teaching methods will improve our standing in international league tables, rather than ask what the purpose of education should be. We endlessly debate about traditional instruction strategies vs. discovery-based learning, rather than identifying what students will need to know, and be able to do, in the new knowledge economy.

This inward-looking insularity comes at a cost. Somewhere along the way, the voices of tomorrow's entrepreneurs – and today's parents – have been lost in the conversation. To give just one example, the way we determine 'what works' in schools is invariably judged by a single yardstick: the performance of students in standardised tests, despite the fact that increasing numbers of employers, universities and colleges are looking elsewhere for more accurate talent indicators. Parents are increasingly withdrawing their children from such tests, teachers are leaving the profession because of them, and students are disengaged, stressed or bored by them. But, to judge by the media response to standardised tests, the only real discussion to be had is whether they've become too easy, or too hard. That is not to say there is no place for tests. It is to say we should be asking ourselves when they are best used and when other assessment methods will serve our children and our economies better.

So, it's our belief that change has to come, and come soon. Of course, in a minority of schools, both in the UK and abroad, change has already come. There are some schools that perform well enough in national standardised tests, but that isn't what drives them. They have worked intensively with parents to make sure their students' wellbeing is paramount. They work with cutting-edge companies to make sure their students engage in real, purposeful, work that matters. And they use technology to support learning that's shaped around the student's passions and individual needs, defying the one-size-fits-all model of education. They don't neglect the fundamentals – literacy and numeracy. Instead, they complement them with digital literacy, oracy, problem-solving, and many other skills that employers are crying out for. They are creating confident, globally-competent, future-ready citizens. If policy-makers have heard of such schools, they seem reluctant to acknowledge that there can be another way, often dismissing attempts to introduce any new approaches as 'fads'.

While we don't give up on the idea of influencing politicians and policy makers, their recent record of listening to education professionals and employers hasn't been at all encouraging. If we're to change the education conversation, it will have to happen through an aggregation of social movements, drawn from a far wider collection of activists than we've seen so far.

We take heart from the number of lobbying groups that are already out there, and it's absolutely not our desire to replace, or compete with, any of them. What we seek is a broad-based coalition of organisations and individuals who feel the time is right to take a positive, forward-looking approach to re-imagining the schools we need in order to best prepare our young people to be future-ready, confident and fulfilled.

Although the provocations you're about to read have a primary focus upon education in the United Kingdom, we know that these issues are commonly situated, and hotly contested, around the world – so we want to hear from our international audience, as well as the domestic readership.

As you reflect upon the ideas in this book, we invite you to ask yourself: 'What does this mean for my students, my business, my community, or my kids?' We believe that the issues raised here affect *all* of us, and are not being sufficiently examined in government, in the media, or around the dining table. But don't stop there. Ask yourself:

'What can be done to bring these concerns to a wider audience, and what can we do to bring about change?

And then get in touch with us – together we can change the conversation.

THE URGENT CASE
FOR CHANGE

CHAPTER 1

Bringing Schools to Life
A Ten-Step Invitation to Engage

by Guy Claxton

Much of the debate on education is superficial and piecemeal. Most policy interventions are just swings of a worn old pendulum: breadth vs. depth, exams vs. coursework, venerable content vs. relevant skills, and so on. In this short piece, we present a more coherent, forward-looking 'manifesto' for school improvement. It contains a critique, a specific vision, a programme for change, and a political and social rationale. You are warmly invited to respond.

Outcomes: Every child deserves a good education, and to feel that they have received one. We think that means they should come out of school knowing how to read, write and do the maths they will all need; enjoying reading and the enrichment that reading gives them; confident with digital technology and understanding something about how it works and its pros and cons; inclined to think critically about what they see and hear; keen to discover and develop their talents and interests; positive, resourceful and imaginative in the face of difficulty and uncertainty; having commitment and pride in a job well done, whatever it may be; and able to engage knowledgeably and articulately with the unfolding political, economic, moral and ecological issues that affect them and their communities. We can and should argue about the details of such a specification, but these are *the kinds of outcomes* that all young people and their families have a right to expect, and schools have a responsibility to develop.

Parents: Our goal is to mobilise public opinion, and especially the voice of parents, families and school students themselves, so that politicians are galvanised into seriously considering deeper policy solutions. Teachers and school principals have to start enthusing parents and pupils about the possibilities of change. There is a welter of concern amongst parents about education. Some children take naturally to academic study and enjoy school. Some, whether they enjoy it or not, have the background, the support and the temperament to be winners at the grades game, but many do not. Millions of parents see school making their children brittle, conservative and anxious in their attitudes to learning, and watch in dismay as their children's adventurous, questing spirit shrivels up and dies, but they do not speak out because they cannot clearly see an alternative. They see it as a family problem rather than a systemic issue. So, reluctantly, many fall back on thinking that the best they can do is help their children suck it up and just do as well as they can on the tests. We need to help parents find a coherent voice for their concerns, one that will have political force. When this clamour reaches a tipping point, the demand for schools that fit children for the real tests of life (and not just for a life of tests) will become irresistible.

Intellectualism: Some – we cannot be sure which – of today's students will become plumbers, mechanics, care workers, singers, shepherds, chefs, upholsterers, jockeys, gardeners, hairdressers, and cartoonists. Some will neither want nor need to go to university. All of them have just as much right to feel empowered by and grateful for their education as those who get good A-levels and go on to become lawyers, lecturers, doctors or business leaders. Some do feel blessed by their schooling, but many do not. Some of them endure the daily experience of feeling inadequate, mediocre or merely bemused by the demands of the curriculum. They feel failures in an education that systematically ignores their interests and devalues their talents. In England particularly, Dance, Design Technology and Physical Education are institutionally less valued than French and History. Children who are not cut out to be scholarly should not be made to feel stupid. There is more complex thinking involved in being a good plumber than a humdrum teacher.

Examinations: High stakes tests are designed and graded so that a substantial proportion of youngsters are condemned to fail – through no fault of their own, no lack of effort, or no inadequate teaching. This is required by a system that is geared to esteem one slim set of academic outcomes above all others. If grades are seen purely as passports to good universities, one child's four A*s at A level only have value because someone else's son or daughter didn't get them. This is unnecessary, unjust, and pernicious. School should genuinely value *all* the kinds of outcomes illustrated above, not just one or two of them. Even for high-achievers, the grades are not all that matter. Grades get students through some narrow gateways and open up valuable options, but once through those gateways, qualities of mind such as perseverance, self-control, curiosity, concentration, and empathy matter more. For example, *pleasure* in reading is a powerful predictor of success in life. Yet the pressure to hit targets of reading *ability* has been shown to undermine children's enjoyment of reading.

Being able to recall information on cue, solve pre-digested problems, and knock out short essays, are not amongst the most important life skills for the 21st century. Curiosity, determination and independent-mindedness matter more and should not be sacrificed on the altar of university entrance. Whatever their path in life, such attitudes and capabilities are the most valuable residues of a child's school-days, and to neglect their cultivation, or worse, to implicitly encourage an attitude of passive, dependent, credulous literal-mindedness is unforgivable. Most schools pay lip-service to wider outcomes, claiming to help their students become happy, confident or equipped for the 21st century', but in the day-to-day learning lives of students these goals are honoured in the breach rather than the observance, and no *systematic* attempt is made to ensure their cultivation. Fond hopes and fine words are inadequate.

Pedagogy: In achieving these vital outcomes, pedagogy – the way that teachers teach – counts for more than the curriculum – the subject matter of their lessons. Of course, acquiring knowledge matters, but attitudes such as scepticism, perseverance or a love of reading cannot be taught directly. Learning *about* running does not (by itself) make you faster. Learning *about* curiosity does not make you more inquisitive. These attitudes are habits of mind that, in a conducive environment, develop and strengthen gradually over time. Teachers can create that culture – the 'nutrient medium for dispositional growth' – through the activities they design, the informal comments they make, the freedoms and responsibilities they offer, the decisions they make about how to lay out the furniture and what to display on the walls, and crucially through the attitudes towards learning they themselves exemplify, especially in the face of unexpected difficulties.

There are clear *design principles for a classroom* that steer students either towards compliant, uncritical, extrinsically-motivated attitudes towards learning; or towards adventurous, critical, proactive attitudes. However, many teachers and school principals are not as conscious and deliberate as they could be about ensuring that their schools and classrooms continually and ubiquitously nurture the latter rather than the former. Some think that teaching style is, provided discipline and achievement are good, an essentially private matter. And some still think, erroneously, that attention to learning skills and attitudes detracts from the development of knowledge and the attainment of good grades. Outstanding schools need to pay constant attention to the 'minute particulars' (as William Blake called them) of teaching method and style.

Knowledge: Though teaching methods are critical for the development of these vital habits of mind, the subjects being studied matter too. You cannot learn to learn in the abstract. You have to learn how to learn in the context of learning *something*. In the midst of a knowledge explosion, however, it is very hard to choose the tiny fraction of all that knowledge that is genuinely useful. The question "What knowledge is likely to matter in the lives that most school students are likely to lead (in the mid to late 21st century)?" needs to be of urgent, widespread concern. In his recent book *Future Wise*, Harvard Professor David Perkins writes: "What's conventionally taught may not develop the kinds of citizens, workers and family and community members we want and need. The basic skills of reading, writing and arithmetic, even if strongly developed, aren't enough. The familiar disciplines…sitting in their silos… taught to all comers for purely academic understanding aren't enough." It is unacceptable to soldier on with the Tudors, simultaneous equations, and the sub-plots in Othello simply because they have been in the curriculum for a long time, or because to grapple with the dizzying array of alternatives makes our brains hurt.

Put simply, there are three kinds of justification for making all young people learn something. First, it – the something – is clearly useful and relevant to the civic, economic and family lives that most people are going to lead. Second, it isn't obviously useful in its own right, but it makes a good exercise machine for developing some general purpose skills and habits of mind that *are* really useful (and which wouldn't reliably be developed by studying things in the first category). And third, neither of the above, but the subject is such a precious cornerstone of our cultural life and heritage that everyone just ought to know about it. People will fight like cats and dogs about what specifically fits into each of these categories, but at least we will be having the right kind of debate.

Evidence: The vital residues of education – useful, portable habits of mind as well as really useful knowledge – need to be documented and demonstrated. School-leavers should be able to evidence their ingenuity or resilience to prospective employers. Conventional tests do not provide this information. It is perfectly possible to do well on many examinations by being a compliant and conservative learner, and to do badly despite being creative and resourceful. Nor do simple check-lists suffice. It would be absurd to send young people out of school labelled and graded in terms of their qualities of mind. Yet there are robust and rigorous ways being developed, often making smart use of digital technology, that do now enable youngsters to evidence their growing capacity and appetite for learning. Parents and employers need to understand what these are, and why they should learn to trust them.

Of course, evidencing the development of dispositions such as curiosity or determination is not as straightforward as marking a maths test. But many existing forms of assessment (e.g. in English or Art) already involve informed judgement on the part of the assessor, and we know there is considerable variation even between expert markers. And yes, some teachers could make unreliable or 'generous' judgments about children's learning dispositions. But demanding ever more draconian kinds of accountability from teachers is not the right way to respond. If we restrict the valued outcomes of education only to those whose evaluations have the appearance of being 'teacher-proofed', the cure is worse than the disease – especially if it makes teachers cautious and defensive, and encourages them to teach to the test or game the system. The only solution is to invest in teachers' ability to know their students at a deeper level. To understand that good grades and lively minds can, but too often don't, go hand in hand, and to know what kinds of evidence of their growth will be valid and reliable. Targeted and sophisticated professional development for teachers is a vital ingredient of the development of 21st century education.

Progress: Within the education profession there is widespread recognition of these concerns, and an increasing number of pioneering schools around the world have developed effective cultures of learning that achieve both aims: students get the best grades of which they are capable, and at the same time they grow in their confidence, capability, and appetite for designing and managing their own learning. Yet the rate at which these beacons of 21st century education are proliferating is still too slow. There are several factors that contribute to this slow rate of growth. Some people still believe that the two aims must necessarily conflict: that attention to developing the qualities of mind must distract (and therefore detract) from the mastery of subject matter. Some are still sceptical about the possibility or desirability of this kind of development in schools. (They may adhere to the idea that intelligence and personality are largely the products of genetics, and therefore beyond the power of teachers to influence.) Some see teaching style itself as largely driven by unalterable traits of personality: 'teachers are born, not made'. Some school leaders see the kudos of their school as dependent only on academic grades, Ofsted ratings (and, perhaps, sporting trophies), and are therefore loath to embrace wholeheartedly a wider set of outcomes. Some still cling (consciously or unconsciously) to the belief that a traditional (grammar) school is the epitome of good education, and that it is just an unfortunate fact of nature that very large numbers of children are simply not equipped with the brain power, the temperament or the family support to benefit from it. These doubts and misconceptions need to be tackled, so that the necessary changes to practice can spread like wildfire.

Politics: Politicians, in particular, are (with a few exceptions) condemned by the short-term, cyclical and tribal nature of most democracies to resist doing what needs to be done to bring about the necessary changes. Their views on education are largely uninformed by anything other than their own school experience, naive intuitions, the entrenched views of powerful media barons, a love of simplistic statistics, and the constantly looming fear of losing the next general election. All of this conspires to make ministers of education, especially, allergic to anything that is subtle, long-term, or easily ridiculed by a cynical editor or journalist. Many senior politicians (ex-lawyers and journalists, often) have also cultivated a debating style that inclines them to rebut sensible questioning with cheap debating points rather than a thoughtful exploration of complex issues. Where research ought to drive policy, instead evidence is cherry-picked and 'weaponised', becoming merely a rhetorical stick with which to beat any argument which they find uncongenial or inconvenient.

There is also a deep resistance by politicians to questioning the fundamental purpose of education; they prefer to talk as if school improvement were a merely technical matter, rather than an indelibly moral one. Thus the driving obsession with improving grades, tests and college or university entrance (especially for young people from disadvantaged backgrounds) goes unexamined. The quality of public debate about education has to be deepened and improved, if desperately needed changes are to stand a chance of scaling up.

A peaceful world. Our world seems to be becoming more turbulent. Mass migrations create stressful uncertainties in migrants, their families and descendants, and often destabilise the traditional communities in which they are seeking to make new homes. Without roots in land, family and tradition, it can be hard to feel valued and significant. But feeling unsettled, anxious and aimless – sometimes even dispossessed or humiliated – can breed a strong desire for certainty, clarity, dignity and purpose that makes people vulnerable to the bogus quick-fix appeal of fundamentalism. Education has to help people strengthen their dispositions to tolerate uncertainty, to think carefully about complex issues, to critique what they hear, and to disagree gracefully. To neglect this poses a threat to the stability and safety of their communities and societies.

Schools that adhere to a traditional curriculum and cultivate an obsession with right answers, however, may inadvertently make matters worse. A Right/Wrong culture can feed what psychologists call a 'need for closure' that makes complexity and uncertainty feel more intolerable, not less. Such teaching methods and school cultures risk encouraging intolerance of other views, which are seen as simply wrong, or worse, bad. In addition, an inflexibly traditional curriculum and factually-based assessment may fail to engage some students – perhaps those who need it most – sufficiently strongly to make them willing to expend the mental energy that would stretch their minds. (To be willing to exercise, you have to *want* to get fitter.)

There is research that underpins these concerns, but they are obviously open to debate. What is beyond question, we think, is that these sorts of concerns are absolutely the right *kinds* of concerns and conversations to be having. Getting education right matters for the wellbeing and fulfilment of millions of individual children and young people; but it is also a larger matter – not just of economy and employment – but of the future of our world.

Guy Claxton is a cognitive scientist with a long-standing interest in education. He has made both practical and academic contributions to education through a series of books that include; *What's the Point of School?*, *Building Learning Power*, *Wise Up: The Challenge of Lifelong Learning*, and (with Bill Lucas) *New Kinds of Smart* and *Educating Ruby*. His latest book, *The Learning Power Approach: Teaching Learners to Teach Themselves*, with a foreword by Carol Dweck, is published in the UK and the US in November 2017. His 'Building Learning Power' approach has been influential in schools in Ireland, Poland, Malaysia, Singapore, Indonesia, Vietnam, China, New Zealand, Australia, Argentina and Chile, as well as across the UK.

CHAPTER 2

The Scrap Heap Challenge

By Mark Stevenson

I imagine a future where a grandchild might come to me and say, "So let me get this right Grandad, when you were young, people used to dig up coal and oil from millions of years ago? And it was dangerous and expensive, and destroyed the landscape, and upset the people where it happened. Then you'd burn it in big buildings to create electricity, or set fire to it to run your engines, but those buildings and engines would lose most of the energy as waste heat? And people used to go to war for the stuff in the ground because everyone wanted it so much, but when you burnt it, it helped kill more people than all those wars put together through pollution and climate change? Did I get that right?"

And I'd have to say, "Yes, that's about it."

"But Grandad," they might say. "That sounds stupid when energy is coming out of the sky for free!"

And I might try to give some context. "Well, we didn't always have the know-how or the technology to get the energy in the way we do now. And when we did work it out, the people who'd built the old system weren't happy about the new one because that's how they paid themselves and fed their families. We'd become very accustomed to that way of doing things. It seemed, er, normal."

To my grandchildren (should I be blessed with any) our energy system will seem ridiculous, short-sighted, barbaric even. Those who resist the shift to renewables may, in retrospect, seem cartoonish in their defense of the old, the easy villains of history – for my grandchildren will have grown up in a different energy culture, one where, in many parts of the world, generating power locally and cleanly will seem obvious and unsurprising, the normal way of doing things.

I know this because I've already seen it. For my last book I researched and visited towns of all sizes who already had, or were in the process of moving over to, renewables. One moment sticks in my mind. In the town of Güssing, South Austria, I was sitting in one of the area's many solar facilities. My guide, the ever jolly Joachim, took me into the control room where he showed me how much local households were consuming and their current bills. "They pay about half the price they would with a utility," he said (and those cheap bills, I found out, included a levy for maintenance costs, explaining why the facility was still in fine working order after nearly two decades of operation).

"Well, everyone must be very happy with *that*," I said. Joachim shrugged. "Not really." I was surprised. 'What's not to like', I thought? But I had misunderstood him. It's not that the locals were unhappy, it's just that they'd been making energy this way for twenty years. In Güssing, cheap, reliable, community-owned, renewable energy is nothing remarkable any more. It was an attitude I came into contact with time and time again. From café owners to public officials, from taxi drivers to shop owners, there was (and is) a belief that there is absolutely nothing strange or unique about the way the town generates and distributes its own power. 'Why would you do it any other way?' is a common refrain. "For us, it's normal," said Joachim. "That's it."

Towns as different as Georgetown, slap-bang in the middle of oil-rich Central Texas (population: 60,000) to Wildpoldsried in Germany (population 2,600) – which generates 5 times the energy it needs thanks to a 20 year transition to renewables – have realised that the world of energy is shifting from one of economies of scale to one of economies of distribution, and, slowly, the smarter national governments of the world are realising it too. Indeed they must if they want to remain competitive. Keeping your old monolithic energy system while trying to compete with a nation that has radically reduced its energy bills (while making the system less vulnerable to attack) is economic suicide.

Juan Enriquez is variously an investor, futurologist, former peace negotiator, author, Harvard academic and businessman. And because of these reasons is a man I like to buy lunch for when I'm in his hometown of Boston. Juan told me, "There will be whole nations who end up on the scrap heap because they don't understand this stuff." But when he talks about "stuff" he's not just referring to the energy transition. He's talking also about the questions the future raises for us about transitioning away from our unsustainable food system (and the related water stress it creates), the impact of artificial intelligence, the power of synthetic (programmable) biology, climate change, the promise and threat of blockchain powered administrations, the ageing of our populations… the list goes on.

Juan is highlighting the importance of what I call 'future literacy' – which I define as: understanding the questions the future is asking us, and then working out how we can answer those questions to make the world more sustainable, equitable, humane and just – for everyone. If nations are, as Juan puts it, to "understand this stuff", they will need future-literate education systems that can comprehend those questions and create a citizenry willing and capable of answering them. In the UK (and in many developed economies) that is not the education system we have. Nowhere near.

There is a staggering lack of future literacy in many of our educational institutions. There is little understanding of the real questions the future is asking us – those our children will be called upon to answer. We teach our students, on the whole, to know things, but not how to ask the right questions. I can vouch for this because I deal with the results of the poor-questioning mind in the workplace. Too often organisations leap to create products, services or policies that answer the wrong question, a superficial one or one that no-one really cares about, including their employees. The Right Question Institute sums the problem up:

> *The ability to produce questions, improve questions and prioritise questions may be one of the most important— yet too often overlooked—skills that a student can acquire in their formal education. However, this skill is rarely, if ever, deliberately taught to students from kindergarten through high school. Most people acquire the skill through exposure to an elite education, or years of higher education, advanced training and much professional experience.*

Why is it not taught? Perhaps because it's hard to assess in the traditional way. And perhaps because the questions we need to ask are considered too dangerous for young minds? Maybe questioning why we have a governance system built for the 19th Century still in place in the 21st isn't something those in charge are keen to discuss. Or why is democracy in decline? Or why public trust has evaporated? Or why inequality is soaring? Or why so much of our press is prejudicial? I'm a fan of Voltaire's maxim: 'Judge a man by his questions rather than by his answers.' If we were to judge the UK's education system by the questions it's asking I fear many of us would find the exercise dispiriting.

A second, and related, problem is that there is precious little systems thinking in education. We split the world into subjects and then complain that our organisations are not agile enough to deal with change. Yet should we be surprised when we build those organisations in the image of the education we had, replacing 'subjects' with 'departments' that rarely talk to each other? The devil, we are told, is in the detail, but the devil is really in the cracks separating fields of expertise that siloise themselves into (non)intellectual bubbles, unable it seems to comprehend the systemic problems we face. Just to be clear, I'm not *in any way* against specialism and mastery. I'm against it being isolated from meaning, context and future literacy (an isolation that some senior academics seem to pride themselves on).

This lack of future literacy and systems thinking has led us to the ridiculous situation in education of championing 'hard' subjects above all others, putting on a pedestal the very skills that the machines outperform us on a thousand times over, all without raising a mechanical eyebrow. Yet the jobs of the future will increasingly demand skills of empathy, collaboration, systems thinking, caring, philosophy, creativity, craft – the very things we call 'soft' subjects. Don't get me wrong, I am a *nut* for the so-called 'hard' stuff (I willingly took Maths, Physics and Economics at 'A' level and graduated top of my year with a Business Technology degree before becoming a cryptography nerd). Judge me on the fact I used to sooth my baby boy to sleep by reading him passages on number theory from *The Principia Mathematica.* And you won't find me arguing against a need for literacy (despite starting that sentence with 'and'). After all, part of my living is writing research-heavy books for a general audience. But to suggest in a world increasingly full of artificial intelligence, big data and robotics, that these skills are where the work (and the fulfilment) will be for most people is madness.

A clear result of these and other problems with our education system is that we have made a good deal of learning *very dull* – which is a hell of an achievement when you think about it. Our children look at the silos, the traditions, the protectionism of an old set of values, and a curriculum that seems wholly unsuited for the world they see around them and become bored or actively antagonistic. If the education system worked, they figure, perhaps the planet wouldn't be heading to environmental collapse and riven with mass inequality, while the powerful continue to defend political systems poorly equipped to deal with the problems we face. The results of a 2012 Canadian study of 63,000 schoolchildren are typical, finding that only 39% of them found lessons engaging. That said, they don't necessarily dislike school. 69% were engaged with its social aspects and, importantly, the *idea* of school – understanding that it's there to help them improve their life chances.[1] In short, kids understand that school is a good idea *in principle* but find lessons boring or irrelevant. It's hard to blame them – and it's a lost opportunity of gargantuan proportions.

But what do we do to schools that dare to experiment, to break through the silos, to embrace systems thinking, to encourage future literacy and, as a result, encourage personal responsibility for making the future better? (In short schools children actually like and value). It seems that our educational overseers soon bully them back to compliance with the old ways. It is a great irony in education that those in positions of power are the ones the old system served well (often thanks far more to socio-economic factors than raw talent) making them *precisely the wrong people* to build a better one. They will soon recreate the system that served them. By the way, I'm one of those that did well, but I'm under no illusion that much of that is down to the accident of my birth (white, male and middle class to loving parents – or 'my big break' as I like to call it). Children from disadvantaged and poor backgrounds don't get the second chances that kids from more affluent households might enjoy (allowing them, for instance, to get a job more easily get a job at the Department for Education or OFSTED, or become futurist authors). Their disengagement, as the US National Research Council puts it, 'increases dramatically their risk of unemployment, poverty, poor health, and

---

[1] What did you do in School Today?: The Relationship Between Student Engagement and Academic Outcomes, by Jodene Dunleavy, J. Douglas Willms, Penny Milton, and Sharon Friesen, Canadian Education Association, September 2012 – http://www.cea-ace.ca/sites/cea-ace.ca/files/cea-2012-wdydist-report-1.pdf

involvement in the criminal justice system.'[2] The cost to our economies is enormous. The human cost unimaginable.

And so to perhaps the biggest problem with education. In the UK (and elsewhere) it has become politicised. 'Traditional' and 'progressive' have become code-words for Right and Left. In the same way renewable energy in the US is seen by some as a 'liberal' idea, so attempts to change the curriculum to embrace a changed world rather than propping up the old one is often cast as the indoctrination of children into a leftist ideology. By the same token, advocacy of discipline or rigour, or suggestion there is a great deal of value in training the memorising muscle is decried by some as the crushing (and politically motivated) hand of conservatism.

Enough.

Depending on what question you need to answer, nearly every approach to pedagogy has its place. But if you're asking the wrong questions, as our education systems are, everyone can point to the failings of everyone else, because *no* approach is sufficient. Society continues to stagger from one crisis to the next, and it's always the other side's fault. So, do we all keep on failing and blaming the other 'side', or can we wake up and jointly create an education system fit for the century we're going to be living in? Because if we

---

[2] Summary of Findings and Recommendations (page 211): Engaging Schools: Fostering High School Students' Motivation to Learn, by Committee on Increasing High School Students' Engagement and Motivation to Learn; Board on Children, Youth and Families; Division of Behaviour al and Social Sciences and Education; National Research Council, The National Academies Press, 2004 – http://www.nap.edu/catalog/10421/engaging-schools-fostering-high-school-students-motivation-to-learn

don't we'll end up vapourising our economy. As Juan said, "There will be whole nations who end up on the scrap heap because they don't understand this stuff."

I imagine a future where a grandchild might come to me and say, "So let me get this right, Grandad … when you were young you used to send kids to school to learn about the world by dividing it up into 'subjects' – just as the world became more connected? And you valued the things you could easily examine even though the machines could do most of them better? And education was about answers not questions, and about individual performance rather than collaboration in the service of the common good? And kids from rich families had more help and opportunity than kids from poor ones? Did I get that right?"

And I'd have to say, "Yes, that's about it."

"But Grandad," they might say, "That sounds stupid, and really boring – and not good for the country!"

And I might try to give some context. "Well, the education system was born in a different time and the people who'd built the old system weren't so happy about a new one because that's how they paid themselves and fed their families. We'd become very accustomed to that way of doing things. It seemed, er, normal."

Nelson Mandela famously said, "Education is the most powerful weapon which you can use to change the world." When I hear this quoted, as it often is in educational circles, I'm surprised that it is always taken in the positive. But education is as much a weapon to change the world for ill as it is for good. Educate a populace into isolationism, deference to the status quo, self-interest over the greater good, compliance over creativity, exam results over social and economic ones and you can indeed change the world – just not in a very nice way.

Finally, shouldn't building a future-literate education system be *fun,* goddammit? Shouldn't we all be throwing our hearts and minds into it with the greatest of enthusiasm, pooling all our different perspectives and experience in a spirit of collaboration, and making new and unexpected friendships along the way? Shouldn't we be modeling something our children can be proud of, rather than sustaining the tribal squabbling that seems to characterise so much of the debate in education? All that achieves is handing the reigns of power to those with the biggest sticks, instead of the best collaborators.

The scrapheap awaits, as does a rebirth. There are consequences to our decisions. Let's not make ourselves the easy villains of history. Let's move education forwards. And let's really *enjoy* doing it.

Self described 'reluctant futurist' Mark Stevenson is the author of two bestselling books, *An Optimist's Tour of the Future* and the award-winning *We Do Things Differently.* He is one of the world's most respected thinkers on the interplay of technology and society, helping a diverse mix of clients that include government agencies, NGOs, corporates and arts organisations to become future literate and adapt their cultures and strategy to squarely face the questions the future is asking them. His many advisory roles include Sir Richard Branson's Virgin Earth Challenge, Civilised Bank and the Atlas of the Future.

CHAPTER 3

What is it for?
Renewing the Purpose of Education

by Valerie Hannon

If education is truly to move forwards, in tune with the times, we have to rethink its purpose. Our current education system, which emerged in the middle of the 19th century, and was designed to serve the needs of the Industrial Revolution, is under intense strain. There is a growing perception that the mass education system is failing the public.

In some senses, there has been a welter of change in education, under the banner of 'school reform'. But these changes have, in truth, been superficial. They have manifestly failed to address the weakness of the public education system.

What are these failings?

- Learner dissatisfaction or disengagement
- The growing costs of the current system with marginal (or flat-lining) gains on existing outcome metrics[3]

---

3 For example: in the US over the last 40 years, the average spending per pupil has doubled (from $4529 to $11,184) but achievement on

- Frustrated, unfulfilled education professionals (who are not treated as professionals)
- Little impact on inequality – indeed, often the reverse
- Profound mismatch with the needs of societies and of economies

Public debates about education – some of which are polarised – have chiefly revolved around a set of issues such as:

what should be taught
how it should be taught
to whom it should be taught
how it should be structured
how it should be paid for

These are all important questions. Perhaps, in times of stability and continuity they are the ones to focus on. However, those are not our times.

The wrong story

The problem stems from the fact that we have not been prepared to ask the fundamental question of what, today, education should be *for* – what job we want the education system to do. There is an implicit assumption that the answer is too obvious to discuss. When politicians state their 'commitment' to education, it usually boils down to two ideas. The first is to promote 'growth' in the national economies: education will lead to bigger GDP. And second, individuals (if they work hard and are clever) will gain advantage in getting access to better jobs.

---

the National Assessment of Education progress has barely moved.

Both these ideas are threadbare. Whilst there is some evidence that in developing countries, higher levels of education lead to improved economies, in the 'developed' nations that relationship is harder to show, since growth and prosperity depend on a wide and inter-related range of factors. But more significantly, what is *growth?* This is almost always equated with GDP – an indicator increasingly acknowledged to be misleading and insufficient.

The common-sense idea that 'more' education will help us to be better off doesn't stand up because the idea that 'growth' is an unquestioned good is profoundly unsound. We have been doubling down on the industrial age mandate for growth above all else. Instead, we should accept that the era of extractive growth in relation to the resources of the planet is over. New thought in economics is pointing to the revised ideas about 'good growth'. And this is actually about *thriving* – not just producing and consuming more and more. But this old taken-for-granted idea that education is about boosting national GDP has turned education into a sort of global arms race.

The second common-sense idea about education is that it will lead to better jobs for individuals. It is assumed to be the passport to higher income and social mobility. To some extent the (UK) data bears this out. A university degree earns you on average £7,000 a year more than not having one. (Though in many cases that premium is reduced by the need to pay off the now substantial levels of student debt accrued). However the reality is that the current education system is predicated on a system of filtering which remains deeply linked to social class – the evidence shows that social mobility has hardly increased at all. Moreover, 'social mobility' as a goal is itself inadequate: it takes for granted a hierarchical system in which inequality is a given. Far from reducing inequality, we see that, everywhere, inequality is actually on the rise. The developments likely to take place in the labour market over the next thirty years, are likely to make competition for good (i.e. satisfying and well paid) jobs even tougher. The rise of under-employment – taking low-level, unsatisfying jobs is making more young people wonder what it was for. In any case, is that the best that education can do in the future – offer a slightly enhanced chance in the jobs race?

There is no clear narrative for public education today that both connects with the realities people are experiencing and faces up to what can confidently be said to be on our horizon. We have some good evidence about the direction and pace of change. It is unlike anything the human species has faced previously. Some of the challenges are existential. All of these will impact our children's lifetimes, let alone our grandchildren. Reflecting on the scale and direction of these shifts, I believe that *today, education has to be about learning to thrive in a transforming world.*

If this is the job we want the education system to do, we need to have a handle on the transformative shifts that are underway. There is an increasingly secure body of evidence on these. It is largely ignored by education.

Change? Really?

Of course the future is unknowable, but we do have an increasing volume of analytical evidence on some clear trends. Naturally these may be impacted by unforeseen events, and (hopefully) by human action. But, as things stand, taken together they mean that today our species and its home planet stand on the brink of changes that, within the lifetimes of today's young learners, will impact upon their very nature. The changes are complex and unprecedented. Professor Klaus Schwab, Founder and Executive Chairman of the World Economic Forum (WEF), set out his view for the WEF in 2016:[4]

> *The changes are so profound that, from the perspective of human history, there has never been a time of greater promise or potential peril. My concern, however, is that decision makers are too often caught in traditional, linear (and non-disruptive) thinking or too absorbed by immediate concerns to think strategically about the forces of disruption and innovation shaping our future.*

There is increasing consensus about the nature of these forces, and what they mean for us. However, 'traditional, linear thinking' is exactly what prevails in education today, which ignores entirely the 'forces of disruption and innovation' and their implications.

The changes can be grouped into 3 categories:

Our Planet's Predicament. With the exception of the diehard climate-change deniers, it is now widely accepted that our planet stands on the brink of profound and uncontrollable change. If greenhouse gas emissions continue to rise, we will pass the threshold (two degrees above pre-industrial levels) beyond which global warming becomes catastrophic and irreversible. This pivot point will result in rising sea levels, polar melting, droughts, floods and increasingly extreme weather. No nation will be unaffected; in fact, some have already begun to feel the effects. But this is not

---

[4] Schwab K. 2016. The Fourth Industrial Revolution. World Economic Forum

all. We are systematically diminishing the bio-diversity of the planet such that scientists have now recognised that we are entering the 6th Great Extinction. Whilst previous extinctions were driven by natural planetary transformations (or catastrophic asteroid strikes), the current die-off arises from human activity. Fifty percent of all species could be extinct by the end of the century. How can humans thrive if our home environment does not?

The Supremacy of Technology. Most people, when they think about the future, go first to the technological revolution. The power and penetration of technology to reshape the world have attained unprecedented levels. Technocratic solutions are assumed to be capable of resolving any and all problems. From the perspective of humans' capacity to thrive, and the role of education, two aspects are of special interest. The first and most obvious is the impact on jobs. The capacity of robots to assume many millions of jobs and tasks currently performed by humans is now unquestioned. The debate lies in the implications of this. Estimates vary: but there is an increasing consensus that the impact will be large and serious. The second aspect of relevance is the rapid developments in artificial intelligence (AI). The prospect of computers that can acquire the capacity to learn will mark a unique juncture in the relationship between our species and its technologies. The idea that human beings are the source of meaning as well as power is about to be challenged. How can we ensure that humans can thrive, as this relationship unfolds and the balance shifts?

Designing our own evolution. The convergence of the life sciences with the digital explosion has created the capacity to reshape the very fabric of life: it is changing not just what we can do, but who we are. The cost of gene mapping has plummeted. Individual gene sequencing will shortly be able to identify the exact nature of a particular cancer and its pathways. Genetic engineering of pigs is taking place to harvest lungs for transplant (and soon hearts and kidneys). Genomic screening and trait selection are advancing. The convergence, through implants or by other means, of human bodies with artificial intelligence is currently being researched. This is sometimes referred to as 'transhumanism' or 'superintelligence'. Nick Bostrom, the leading thinker in this field, argues persuasively that the future impact of artificial intelligence is perhaps the most important issue the human race has ever faced: the potential for designing our own evolution. It is entirely possible that human beings are not at an evolutionary end point, but that we are destined to evolve further, playing a major role in the design and direction of the process.

All of these are evidence-based shifts which are currently well underway. They are not fantasy or science fiction and *our children will have to live with them* – or, learn to shape them.

The key response for our generation must surely be to debate the implications of these changes thoughtfully, and craft an educational response adequate to the challenge. In the UK, and many other systems, it has not even started.

I suggest that as a starting point, if we can agree that *education has to be about learning to thrive in a transforming world,* then we at least have some basis for the debate. The question then becomes: what might 'thriving' look like?

Learning to Thrive

When we examine what it means to thrive, we see that thriving must happen at 4 interdependent levels, none of which can be ignored:

global – our place in the planet
societal – place, communities, economies
interpersonal – our relationships
intrapersonal – the self

Planetary/Global thriving

Collectively and individually, we have to learn to live within the earth's renewable resources. This entails not just learning how to redirect new technologies, but also to be responsible consumers, and how to reshape economies so that they are not predicated on endless growth and limitless consumption. This geo-political problem is also a learning challenge: for new generations must re-make their relationship with the physical planet. Similarly, the acquisition of global cultural competence, in the sense of respectful appreciation and tolerance, is the only means by which we can create the conditions for peace. The experience of globalisation is now profound and extensive. It now has many critics, but they will have to learn how to reshape it, since it is unlikely to disappear.

National/local thriving

Whilst the nation-state may be eroding, learning how to reinvent democracy into some more participative process will be increasingly important if aspirations for equity and progress are to be realised. There is widespread dissatisfaction or disinterest in instruments of governance. If the collective learning is to create new means and processes for participative democracy, then at the individual level, the challenge is to learn how to practise it – and understand its importance. As economic turbulence and restructuring proceed apace, learning to earn a living through 'the start-up of you' must gain centre stage. In our increasingly longer lives, we must learn to expect and embrace change of job, career, field, skill-set – not once but regularly. And as economies will increasingly depend upon entrepreneurship and creativity, so too will individuals, both for material wellbeing and their own satisfaction. The processes of learning and earning will become symbiotic. So, as there will be no sharp distinction in start- and end-points of education and work, learning's purpose and function will be intrinsic to working life. Learning to make a living successfully and contribute to the new economies will entail learning to think and act 'green, lean, and eco'. It will also mean learning to adapt to work with automation, and with co-workers who are robots.

Interpersonal thriving

The evidence is clear-cut. The finding of the most extensive longitudinal study of adults ever[5] is simple: "good relationships keep us happier and healthier". As we become more reflective (and knowledgeable) about the conditions for, and skills involved in, creating and maintaining healthy human relationships, we recognise the scope for *learning* in this space. The damage done to individuals through dysfunctional families; the scarring of societies by sexist and racist behaviours – from atrocities to discrimination – is incalculable. Again, fast-changing conditions in this century increase the urgency for

---

[5] The Harvard Study of Adult Development. See http://www.adultde-velopmentstudy.org

education to address this cluster of challenges. Changes to family structures, multicultural communities, provide the diverse contexts within which learning to relate authentically, and respectfully takes place. Education needs to equip learners with the knowledge base and the skills to acquire empathy and insight. Engagement in the arts of all forms is one route for achieving this. Though digital technologies in learning are a liberating force, they have also created the spectre of the 'new Mowglis' – brought up by screens, unsocialised and isolated. In an age when immersion in digital environments has been responsible for the pornographication of sex, compounding grotesque sexism, it is a challenge for learning to enable people to acquire sexual identities which do not harm; but rather enhance and humanise life. Finally, learning to care for and nurture others must in the future extend well beyond family ties: demographic changes are creating aged societies, few members of which will remain healthy and independent till death.

Intra-personal thriving

Learning about and within our own selves presents the ultimate frontier – and for some thinkers is the precondition for authentic learning in other domains. But in the C21st the notion of 'self' will change; humans will have access to more and more forms of enhancement (physical and cognitive). Humans must learn to deal with exponentially increased levels of artificial intelligence applied to everyday life; to a gradual incorporation into our own bodies of powerful technologies. Life journeys will be much longer, centenarians not unusual. Taking early personal responsibility for health and fitness will be a precondition for later wellbeing (in addition to preventing the collapse of health systems because of lifestyle illnesses like the obesity epidemic). Dignity, purpose and social engagement will be the dividends of continuing to learn. And lastly, the spiritual dimension cannot be omitted. Increasingly, in mechanised, technology-infused, confusing modern life, the need for mindfulness, awareness, inner silence and balance is becoming more acute. Organised learning must provide the means for its acquisition. There are many routes: the joy of the arts is one. Ultimately however, we cannot avoid the conclusion that there is an enduring response to this question of learning's purpose. It consists in *wisdom* – though redefined for our post-modern context.

What would bringing these imperatives in to the *centre* of our learning goals, instead of at the periphery, look like? Something like this perhaps:

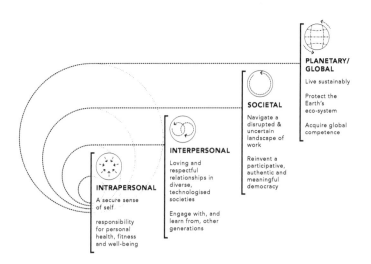

And there are visionary educators in schools across the world who are doing just that. In the UK, the system conditions are set firmly against such a direction because there is no public leadership able to articulate a new purpose for education.

Where are the politicians who will face this?

The public debate around education (in the UK especially, but not exclusively) is truly pitiful. The agenda ranges from "bring back the grammars, the selection, knowledge-transmission!" from one political wing; to "more money!" (for the same-old, same-old) at the other. Yet radical redesign is needed, and it is urgent. There will only be an appetite for this when education's *purpose* is refreshed. Where are the politicians who can start to shape and frame that debate? To be sure, they face an uphill struggle. Vested interests and the media collude to maintain an echo-chamber which constrains how people can think about these issues. Many parents, given the space to reflect and consider the challenges, are profoundly discontented with the current offer. And a number of systems around the world are starting to show how shift can be achieved. Crucially, there are now numerous examples of schools demonstrating how a futures-oriented set of purposes can be transformational for their learners.

In such schools the dimensions of learning stay the same: they address knowledge, skills, dispositions and values. Of these, values have been the least considered in conventional systems, and yet are perhaps the most critical. We should ponder the fact that Goebbels had a PhD in literature. And the people who caused the financial crisis of 2008 were not 'uneducated'.

The year 2016 saw a sea-change across Europe and the US of political culture, with global implications: the rise of successful populist demagoguery, relying on 'post-truth' campaigns, signalling the howl of exclusion and impotence that large sections of those populations experience. But education continues with the old prospectus: the promise of 'succeeding' (gaining better competitive access to the shrinking pool of good jobs) if the right knowledge and skills are acquired. Many have seen how hollow this promise has been. Educators can't struggle with creating a different debate and a new prospectus alone. It's time for a new generation of politicians to create a fresh narrative and new possibilities.

Valerie Hannon is an established thought leader in the field of education innovation. Valerie co-founded Innovation Unit (UK and Australia). She is a founding member and Co-Chair of the Global Education Leaders Partnership (GELP) supporting jurisdictions globally to scale their innovation and transform their systems. Valerie is an expert adviser on education to the OECD, and a frequent contributor to the World Summit on Innovation in Education (WISE). She is a regular keynote speaker and facilitator at international conferences and workshops. Her latest book is *THRIVE: Schools Reinvented for the Real Challenges We Face* is now available on Amazon (IUP 2017).

MAKING A DIFFERENCE

Parents, Pedagogy, Knowledge and Intellectualism

CHAPTER 4

Moving the Curriculum Forwards

by Mick Waters

One way of looking at what we will need for the future is to imagine getting to the future and looking backwards. If today's children, starting school in, say, 2020 were to look in the rear-view mirror and reflect on their schooling in the year 2050, would they be pleased with what they had learned?

Some future challenges

By 2050, how will the world have changed? The opportunities and challenges we currently face might influence what young people should learn. In the developed world, we have an ageing population with a growing proportion of people taking human life beyond the limits we knew a century ago. In thirty years' time, will we have found a cure for some of the illnesses of increasing age? The gap between rich and poor is destined to grow and the shift of people across the globe will increase rather than subside. By 2050, will the capacity to pipe water to Africa be matched by the will to do it and so release a vast amount of the world's land surface as a productive resource? How far will humans toil physically and will robots have taken over the processing of much of the human condition? Our knowledge of the human brain is expanding at such a rate that we might be able to address disorder and improve capacity. Will the superpowers of today be the superpowers of the next generation? Will China and India be the economic giants? Will the States still be united? To what extent will the climate have changed and how far will we be able to generate energy to support the planet without destroying its very existence? Technology will have expanded its reach; in communication, logistics, design, transport, war, commerce and finance, touching every part of our lives.

These are big picture questions. Our children are growing into a world that offers greater opportunity than ever before and, at the same time, some challenges that the adults before them have never met, let alone addressed. At the same time, most would want our children to be growing up to take their place in society as responsible adults, able to manage their own lives and contribute. Indeed, in just a few short years after moving to secondary education, our children will be old enough to be employed, in business, in the military, married and parents. Most would want them to be decent members of society. The thought that any of them could be asked to be a juror should be salutary for every teacher. The thought of being faced with an ex-pupil across the court (it couldn't happen in reality) might make every teacher think, 'I'd better teach the ability to weigh an argument, to discern fact from supposition, to make reasoned decisions.'

Of course, whatever the future holds, our society will still need some people to work out how to feed us all, to construct, to clean up the messes we create. We will need those who tend to the sick, bring succour and compassion. There will be a need for those who entertain and amuse along with those who help to enact laws that some of us make or defend the principles that we hold against those who might oppose us. The belief that schools should fuel the economy and provide the nation's workforce has traditionally influenced our thinking on what should be taught but, in truth, we need much more.

Some see the school curriculum as a sort of sieve which gradually sifts out those who can do things from those who cannot; the curriculum as a search for talent so that we find the best to supply our universities or our football academies or our ballet schools. Others see the curriculum as a route to social mobility, believing that success in examination will overcome the influence achieved by social networking. Others see the curriculum as opening doors for young people to a world that they will never experience otherwise; to culture, arts, thinking, even books.

At the same time, most would want children to grow up with extended innocence for as long as possible. Childhood should be a joyous time; the endless new experiences, excitement at finding and doing new things, the wonder of the world in which we live in, its scale, nature and beauty. Again, most would want their children protected from the worst of society and the perils that can befall them. From being healthy, to preventing accident or illness, to avoiding influences of perceived evil, most want children to be taught to be wary.

A battleground of ideas and purpose

It is this complexity of ambition for our young that makes devising a curriculum so difficult, especially if we are not clear about the real purpose of our schools. The early chapters of this book highlight the confused and disputed purposes that sway education policy and so often these disputes show themselves in the curriculum, becoming a battleground for ideas. When we add to our considerations the range of views on how people best learn, we complicate the expression of the curriculum. We further complicate things by deciding to measure certain aspects of learning as measures of school and personal success in the form of exams and tests.

It is hard, therefore, to unscramble the complexity of today in trying to state what a school curriculum should be for tomorrow. We usually start with trying to modify the curriculum that is in place and negotiating some change, which leaves the radical reformers disappointed and the traditionalists disheartened, so that each goes away to regroup and return at the next possible opportunity to the battleground of ideas.

The battleground is always busy with skirmishes where people work on unproductive polarities. They refuse to accept that it is possible to teach traditional subjects and more future-focused disciplines. They cannot perceive that we can teach knowledge alongside skills and attitudes. They decline to see that scholarly learning works with practical understanding and vice versa. They prefer not to see that academic and vocational studies can complement each other. There are others in the battlefield who prefer to seek a world of little challenge; of dumbing down, of trendy ideas and gimmicks, giving our young an experience that does not extend them, fails to open doors to new experience and leaves them bereft of much learning.

The rear-view mirror

What would children of today looking in that rear-view mirror want to see in terms of their time at school and what they learned? Surely, they would want to reflect that their schooling had offered a rounded and full experience that prepared them for the complex lives they have enjoyed and face?

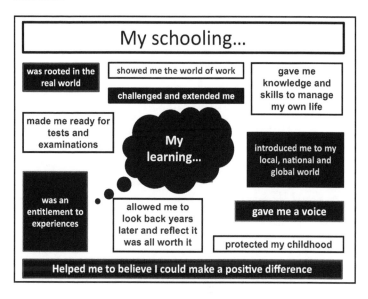

Different learners; different needs

Those people looking back might reflect that the school managed to get the balance right between what they had learned at home with their parents, what they learned in their communities and what the school itself needed to provide. Indeed, if the main things that young people need to learn are about being able to function effectively in everyday life; to tell the time, manage money, read, be able to hold conversations for various purposes and use the internet, then surely by now in an educated society it should be easy enough to do all this without going to school? Does there really need to be a formal experience of schooling so that children will get on with others, learn to adopt a healthy lifestyle and not fall into bad ways? Yet often, the school is seen as the place where these basic tenets for life will be acquired. At other times, there is a move towards expecting schools to develop in the young outlooks that the adults find hard to manage. Dealing with equalities, or enabling communities to co-exist where there is traditional suspicion is the sort of thing that is often laid at the door of the school. It is often suggested that such issues as radicalisation, genital mutilation or religious bigotry should be addressed with children in schools. Hence, often, the school is the starting point for the solution to the exasperations of 'young people these days... can't... won't...always...don't; schools should...'. The list for schools extends to ensuring the best for youngsters in terms of everything from work readiness, to personal finance, to grooming, sexting, dental health, radicalisation, and voting.

At the same time, we need to be able to find youngsters who can go on to work at a high level of understanding. We need people to do the complex jobs and to push the boundaries of understanding through research. From basic function to world-changing invention, can schools prepare the young for all of it at once?

If we take an example of learning about health, we somehow have to find ways of enabling all youngsters to understand, say, the importance of their vital organs and how to protect them from harm and protect society from the health cost of negligence while at the same time helping the appropriate youngsters to study the human anatomy to a level which will eventually provide the medical care for the needy. At the same time, we need to find the people who are destined to develop new solutions to the challenges of maintaining health and reducing or curing illness.

Curriculum complexity, distortion and confusion

It is this search for balance that is often the cause of tension in the battlefield of the curriculum. For many, the curriculum in school is the 'top up' for a full, productive and happy life. Their children have secure home lives and enjoy rich experiences with a learning attitude to the fore. For them, school is the place where the more complex concepts of individual subjects are inculcated. The curriculum in school is an interesting repertoire of learning that provides the qualifications necessary to enter work. For others, school is a proving ground, the make or break that will take children towards better life prospects through qualification. In some cases though, children are coming to school, not needing a 'top up' but nearly on 'empty'. The school is expected to provide the very basics in hygiene, health, personal and social learning, even language as well as the qualifications. Because the purpose of school is unclear, tensions persist.

At the root of all this is whether the school experience 'belongs' to the individual or to society. Perhaps we should accept that it belongs to society and should be tempered to meet the needs of each individual. Some people have greater challenges to cope with in terms of disadvantage or special needs, some have special talents and abilities. If it belongs to the child, then entitlement becomes a key principle and some children might get more than others in terms of meeting their more extensive needs. Nobody is fixed; the ambition of learning is for growth. Words like 'ability', 'performance', and 'potential' should open rather than close possibilities in learning. If it belongs to society then, in a democracy, we would expect schools to teach children some of the central tenets of living together and how society functions. The problem with this standpoint is that this outlook works best when society is at ease with itself; when society is divided there is dispute about the extent to which children should be taught about injustice and social division and schools risk being accused of indoctrination. A fairer, more just world always sounds good until it means a change of power base.

Next, we might question whether we need a national curriculum that details the learning that will be set before children. We need to free curriculum from the political tugs of war and allow it to be broadly defined by a wider community of interest. The detail of subject disciplines can surely be left to experts. Indeed, the time has surely come for international collaboration on how to teach concepts. Trigonometry, algebra, density, latent heat and glaciation are the same the world over; it is surely possible to construct modules of study to enable learning to what we call A level standard. The studies of things like literature and the history of art should be globally influenced and we have surely moved past the point where we think that we can select but a few authors, poets or artists as 'the essentials' for every learner.

Currently we have a national curriculum which is designed to accelerate a minority of children to supposed success at sixteen with the promise of further success at A level. Its problem is that it also risks disenfranchising many children and creating negative learning outlooks, attitudes and beliefs. Why is this? It is because one way of trying to squeeze 'performance' out of schools is to put pressure on teachers to produce rather than children to learn. We set exams where the proportion of passes at each grade is fixed and then make schools fight over whose pupils get the pickings.

Too often, we make learning abstract and separate from the real world. Learners are invited to climb ten parallel subject ropes with the clear assumption that many will only be able to completely climb a few and then only half way. For most learners, the announcement that they are 'no good' at certain subjects is a given, even when they achieve GCSE. It is a strange phenomenon that children enter school knowing little history and we teach them until they announce they cannot do it. It is hardly success.

People might need 'courses of study', including those in traditional subjects. A linear programme covering aspects of subjects and demonstrating competence through an exam is one way to learn. At present though, learners have to do nine or ten of these for two or maybe more years as they climb their separate ropes towards GCSE. The courses are too long. It should be possible to pass a GCSE in science in a short time if the basic understandings and knowledge are secure prior to the introduction of a specific syllabus for the examination. As it is, with the high stakes accountability regime for schools built upon annual results, the syllabus is stretched to provide more time on the practice and the learning is focused upon rehearsing for an exam.

The narrowing of focus is also prevalent at primary schools. What gets tested and inspected gets taught; literacy and numeracy dominate. Too many children experience little art, dance, drama, music, even history and geography become another vehicle for literacy. Science lacks experiment for so many children. There are plenty of so called outstanding schools elsewhere where the life blood is sucked out of learning to sustain high test scores.

We might need to question some of the traditions of schooling. The timetable, lessons themselves, exercise books for each subject, marking, the way teachers are observed and therefore expected to work – these are all aspects of learning that are only slightly developed since schools were set up centuries ago. When we give every pupil an exercise book for their subject, do we not communicate that learning is an isolated activity, based in exercise, which can only be covered as the teacher unfolds the next page? In the real world of science, upwards of a thousand people contribute to a paper on physics. In astronomy, the number of contributors rises to 3,000 and in genetics it is often 10,000, and even more comment upon it. Yet we expect our young to 'do their own work', and someone else, called 'a teacher', marks it. Perhaps we need to think differently for the future.

A curriculum for the future?

Where might we start to develop a curriculum for the future? First, we should expect every school to make maximum use of every moment that is available. The curriculum is the entire planned learning experience. It includes the lessons and so much more. The daily life of school, its routines, will teach children much. The events that a school arranges will teach more. What children do beyond the 'school day' will be productive for learning if well used. For the curriculum to prepare children to face the future, it needs to speak to children positively at every point. There is much talk about raising aspiration in young people; this is far more than helping children to believe that they can 'be anything that they want to be', far more than achieving high grades or reaching higher levels. *Aspiration*: at the root of the word is 'spirit' and the curriculum should be about aspiration of spirit, of contribution and worth. If society is to be effective and people are to be fulfilled, it is their spirit and outlook on life that will be as vital as the knowledge and skills they acquire. Indeed, important knowledge and skills are more likely to develop when worth and spirit are secure.

Learning with purpose

Children and young people need to think their study has a purpose, hence the need to think about the rear-view mirror. How can we provide a curriculum that entices, absorbs, challenges, stretches and gives purpose? Does that need to be done nationally? Is it not possible for the community of a school, rather than the nation, to determine what it wants for its learners?

How would we describe a good curriculum?

A good curriculum emphasises the inter-relatedness of concepts, big ideas, critical thinking and learning that is personalised to respond to the differences in individuals. It includes foundation skills in literacy and numeracy, coding and associated logic, personal responsibility and self–awareness and assessment.

Learning is based on enquiry, project- and problem-based learning, using research skills and scientific methods. Flexibility of learning environments is encouraged, including involvement with the community and experience of the world of work. International perspectives are natural, local interpretations of study are accessed and theoretical perspectives explore some abstract learning.

It is the complexity of the previous two paragraphs that seems to unsettle many people. When described in this way, it sounds complicated. The simple polarised arguments and comparisons with our own schooling are much safer.

A good curriculum is exciting, dynamic and complex. We are not afraid of it and do not resort to trying to control it by creating models that restrict, reduce and flatten learning. We delight in learning that is sometimes unpredictable and can cope without the need to measure and test everything.

So, what would be the features of a curriculum for the future? A curriculum for the future would:

- encourage a global outlook
- be about doing learning with others
- help understandings of the disciplines of subjects
- be about absorbing through doing
- teach children that learning is worth it
- see learning as something done by communities
- expose and enrich talent
- enable those with difficulty or disability
- emphasise compassion as much as competition
- leave learners wanting more learning in a world where learning was limitless
- see learning as a gift rather than a trial
- make learning irresistible.

Mick Waters is Professor of Education at Wolverhampton University. Each year he spends time in many schools across this country and abroad helping teachers and leaders to develop their practice. He applies his insights to policy work for governments in teaching, curriculum or leadership. He contributes to major conferences, writes extensively and is often to be found in classrooms working with pupils. Mick's ideals are driven by unquenchable optimism, unflinching challenge and realistic recognition of what schools are and could be. He is a trustee or patron of several organisations, all devoted to bringing learning alive and making schooling fit the needs of a global society today and in the future.

CHAPTER 5

Awakening Adventure/ Liberating Imagination

by Hywel Roberts and Debra Kidd

"You dig deeper and it gets more and more complicated, and you get confused, and it's tricky and it's hard, but... It is beautiful."

Professor Brian Cox

"My head hurts when we have to think this hard."

Aisha, aged 7

Under the Bridge

All curriculum starts off as a cold, dead, and to some, alien, document. It's then up to teachers to turn it into something that will resonate with them and their pupils. There are two approaches to this curriculum conundrum. The first is, we just take what we see as coverage, deliver it and hope some of it sticks. This could be labelled as a *cold* approach – one where the awful invisible force-field of stress and despair sneaks up and takes hold of the teacher, robs them of their professional imagination and instinct, and leaves them as hollow deliverers of bullet point scripts and cold coverage.

This is bleak. That's why it's cold. So, what's the contrast? Well, the cold curriculum document needs *warming* up and it really is as simple as that. This document needs wrapping up with stuff that will liberate professional imagination and instinct. It needs humanity. It needs the nettles and barbed wire pulled away from it so that it can be shared and negotiated by children and their teacher-Sherpas. It needs to be a vehicle of knowledge and skill, of course. But the curriculum also needs to be a carrier of meaning for children – a lens through which they can see the world and figure out their place in it. And also learn grammar and that.

So, we're in a Year 1 classroom. It's raining outside and we're all pleased to be indoors. In this moment, Debra is a troll and Hywel is a billy goat. A big billy goat. He's been eating all the stuff and it's causing havoc: the flowers, the vegetables for the Summer Fete, the washing off the washing line – even the trampoline in the garden, according to one young witness. He's a proper greedy billy goat. And what's more, he's a bully goat. And that's the worst kind of billy goat there is.

Our young helpers have been trying to persuade the terrified troll to come out of the shed he is hiding in for ages. And he won't. He's not for shifting. He's frightened of the big goat that pushed him off the bridge and left him to drown. Debra, speaking as the sad-eyed troll, has told them exactly how the billy goat has made him feel.

So when that big old goat comes swaggering into the classroom, patting down his tummy, there's quite a reaction.

"Get out of here you bully. You nasty bully!" cries one child. Interestingly, the child has the beginnings of a smile on his face as he says this. That's because he knows this is *fiction*. He speaks with the authority of someone defending the bullied troll, and he knows in twenty minutes it'll be lunchtime and time for football. Unlike a lot of grown ups, he is more than happy to suspend disbelief and fight the darkness – just like when he plays Minecraft on a night.

Another child moves forward and pushes the billy goat. It's all getting a bit out of hand. Other children rush forward – if pitchforks were to hand, they'd be waving them, like in those old Frankenstein movies. Or in a Twitter storm. As it is, they are waving their fists. Hywel, who has spoken as the cruel old billy goat, beats a hasty retreat to the headteacher's office and makes a formal complaint. Actually, to get a brew.

We hadn't planned for this, you see. We thought they might be a little angry. The idea was to get the two sides talking. Work out how they could live together in peace. We hadn't quite planned on a riot. The teaching assistants are sitting with their pens poised and eyebrows raised. The troll comes out of role to unpick what just happened.

"Well, that frightened him away. I felt a bit sorry for him, didn't you?" says Debra.

"He deserved it!" We're faced with a sea of jaws set in defiance. Then the head walks in.

"I've just had a billy goat in my office. He's very shaken up. He – and I can't quite believe this – says he was pushed by the children in this room. That they shouted at him. Is this true?"

There is silence for a moment. Some eyes are glued firmly to the floor. But some remain resolute.

"But he's a bully. He's been bullying our friend the troll. And eating everything. He deserved it. He's nasty."

"What do we do in our school when someone is mean or doesn't behave how we want them to?"

The head's voice is quiet and calm. He is really good at this stuff. He pauses and then says, "We try to talk and find out what the problem is."

And with beautifully measured emphasis, "We're kind."

There are murmurings and a child puts up her hand. "We never hit each other or push."

The head nods sagely, "So why would you push our visitor?"

There is another long silence. Then the child who pushed first speaks up.

"Is he still here? Can we say sorry?"

The head smiles. As it happens the startled and regretful billy goat appears in the doorway. The TAs smile. All is clear and we are back in the saddle.

Moments later, the class is busily designing and building living quarters for the troll and the goats so that they can live in the village without disrupting each other. They are thinking about building materials, fences, signs, ways to keep some environments damp and others dry. They're considering growing food, drawing designs roughly to scale. They are reflecting how two very different people can live side by side in peace and harmony. They are learning what we intended for them to learn. But they've learned a good more besides. And, don't worry, there will be writing.

The cold flipside to this warm approach is simple to imagine: a depressing worksheet from a mass produced photocopiable resource that tells the story of the Three Billy Goats Gruff and is punctuated by a disappointing illustration that children will be invited to colour in, alongside a box of tasks that encourage children's passive imagination and dull, developing articulacy.

Helping children to make mistakes and learn from them, whilst embracing unpredictability, dilemma and uncertainty, are a critical part of creating adventurous classrooms. And it demands that we too, as teachers, are adventurous and prepared to take risks – to make mistakes. If we fail to open up possibilities for alternatives – even if those alternatives take us to uncomfortable places – we are failing to teach children that life is not predictable and certain. That pathways are not always straight and the dark cul-de-sacs of curriculum possibilities need to be explored and navigated. And it's us, in our roles of teachers and leaders, who are the Sherpas to this wonderful mystery.

"The children have never fallen for my nonsense."

Boris Karloff

Hywel Roberts is a teacher, writer and educationalist working with many organisations across the UK and beyond. He contributes to University Education programmes and is Associate Director of *Independent Thinking Ltd.* A true northerner, Hywel Roberts deals in curriculum liberation, botheredness, creative practice, investment in learning, leadership, teacher development and imagineering in all settings. Hywel also practices what he preaches in classrooms in the UK and abroad, most recently working with The National Galleries of Scotland and The West Yorkshire Playhouse in Leeds. Hywel was recently described as 'a world leader in enthusiasm'. Hywel's award winning book *Oops! Getting Children to Learn Accidentally* is published by Crown House Publishing. His next book, *Unchartered Territories,* written with Dr Debra Kidd, will be published in late 2017. He writes a regular column in the TES.

Debra Kidd has worked in education for 25 years, teaching children from the ages of four to post-graduate in mainstream and special settings. An Associate for the RSA and for Independent Thinking Ltd, she is the author of two books: *Teaching: Notes from the Frontline'* and *Becoming Mobius.* A third with Hywel Roberts, *Uncharted Territories: Great Adventures in Learning,* is due out at the end of the year. She is a columnist for Teach Primary and a regular writer for Teach Secondary and co-founder and organiser of Northern Rocks – one of the largest teaching and learning conferences in the UK. She has a doctorate in Education, blogs regularly and believes more than anything else that the secret to great teaching is "Make it Matter".

CHAPTER 6

The Socially Connected Teacher

by Ross Morrison McGill

Before

The rise of social media services has contributed to the altering of many people's communication patterns and social interaction. Over a decade ago, educators in certain parts of the world, created user profiles on platforms such as Facebook and Twitter without really knowing what it was for, or how they would end up using these forums. According to Twitter Power 3.0[6], today we "send more than 500 million tweets per day … and 6 billion hours of video content each month". That's a huge amount of conversation and opinion, now digitised. Before this epoch, teachers were restricted to connections with colleagues – largely, face-to-face or at best, with two or three others working in nearby schools. Most, myself included, relied upon what little online media there was available at the time, or took for granted what was peddled in the outstanding teaching pamphlets hand-delivered into our staff pigeon-holes from trusted professional development providers. Today, a quick status update during a lesson is very much the future-focused teacher's modus operandi.

Since 2008, I have been sharing content as Teacher Toolkit on various online platforms. When I first searched

---

[6] Comm, J, Taylor D, Kawasaki G, *Twitter Power 3.0* Wiley (2015)

for a range of people to follow, I also hoped that someone would start to follow my updates too. Ten years later, after hours of engaging with others in forums, sharing resources and ideas, I have surpassed all my social media expectations. As I write, I am connected to a learning platform at the touch of a fingertip, with feedback offered at any given moment from the biggest staffroom in the world. This online hub can shape dialogue and challenge policy, and with this new found transparency comes greater accountability. The humble classroom teacher can now generate a dialogue that trends across the UK. I can access immediate feedback from 250,000 colleagues on various platforms quicker than I can secure any commentary in a workplace.

Social media is also replacing the traditional methods of professional development. Free online networks provide support to thousands of teachers across the world. With one click, an informal conversation leads to a grassroots teacher-development event and sooner or later, the digital-savvy educator can curate 500 people, congregating into one room after working hours to share ideas and discuss how they can become a better teacher. In many ways, we churn out 'what we are doing' or 'what we have been doing' updates, with photographs and views about locations and other benign activities, wondering if anyone reads them, never mind if they will connect. The evidence is clear – people do respond.

My first tweet from @TeacherToolkit was in August 2010. The account was always intended to share ideas; an amalgamation of 'Teacher' advice and a 'Toolkit' of resources. Yet, despite already using Twitter from a personal account, in 2008 there was an increasing conflict of interest between sharing personal information and sharing professional work from the same account. Therefore, I made a conscious decision to separate the two. However, this decision may not be for everyone. I still offer work views on an educator account from the position of professionalism and transparency. I write frequently to offer tips for teachers on how to manage your social media profile, but I now keep personal updates separated from work or that of my employer. This is a personal choice and something only you can decide. But do consider when contemplating future job applications, that potential employers now trawl through social media sites to cross-reference the information not included on a CV, noting any vitriol offered to any connected colleagues and establishments.

Today

In 2011, with a specific focus on teaching, reflection and building up online relationships with other teachers, I started to truly understand and discover the potential of social media, observing a pedagogical-shift. The social-media generation began to out-date policy-makers, because thousands and thousands of educators were congregating online, using web-tools to consolidate beliefs and shift thought into personalised co-created professional development circles. Here are just two striking examples. Our school was an early TeachMeet host. TeachMeets are highly social pop-up professional development events. There are now countless TeachMeets being curated by classroom teachers all over the UK, and internationally. Another important example, is of a small group of bloggers – myself included – challenging OfSTED (the Office for Standards in Education, Children's Services and Skills in

England) policy. Nicknamed 'The Famous Five' and the first of its kind, we were invited into Aviation House in London for a roundtable meeting to discuss workload, retention and policy updates, contributing to future policy being 'sampled' before being published to the profession. Today, this process of consulting teachers in some form is thankfully now commonplace.

Teachers are no longer working alone in their classrooms. We can all share ideas, meet together on our terms and critique each other without fear of retribution or job loss. A decade later, teachers are engaging with others in multiple forums, sharing resources and ideas with research-informed examples, citing social media as evidence for new friendships, career moves and alternative income. Hundreds of thousands of teachers, demonstrating something today which is entirely normal, perhaps expected: how teachers use social media to enhance their professional development in the classroom.

In "The $100 Startup" by Chris Guillebeau[7], 'skill transformation' is highlighted as a renaissance for solopreneurship. The word 'teacherpreneur' has been bandied about online for a number of years now, with teachers, notably in the USA and South Korea gaining 'celebrity status' for their online profiles and resource sharing via YouTube and other downloadable mediums to offer resources for others. Guillebeau says, "teachers are usually good at more than just teaching; they're also good at things such as communication, adaptability, crowd control, lesson planning, and coordinating among different interest groups. Teaching is a

---

[7] Guillebeau, C *The $100 Startup: Fire Your Boss, Do What You Love and Work Better To Live More* (2015) Pan

noble career on its own, but these skills can also be put to good use in building online networks."

However, it is not all positive. In recent years, a trend has begun to emerge where high-profile educators engage in calling out other colleagues over their expressed views. Tribalism means that ad hominem attacks from like-minded educators are beginning to undermine the early benefits of supportive critique for the individual, driving some teachers away. I've experienced a number of these attacks, but I've taken a personal decision to continue to connect and remain 'future-focused', despite wellbeing risks and criticism.

We are all empowered to share our knowledge of teaching and learning: what works and what we do not think works in the classroom. We are a by-product of the education system, and we all have our opinion, and with mental health issues increasing our FOMO (Fear Of Missing Out) and the need to be forever connected there is a flipside to the connected professional. With connectivity, comes the disconnect. With online relationships, stems IRL (in real-life) detachment. Equally, it takes a lifetime to build up one's reputation and career repertoire, yet with the virality of social media, just one click or foolish update to throw it all away and tarnish your reputation.

Thankfully, organisations, politicians, schools and teachers have stepped up to the plate and these platforms will allow established users to see the benefits come full-circle – returning to supportive critique. As a teaching (online) community, we have only just started to realise the power of collaboration. Bloggers, tweeters, vloggers (those who use video to diarise) can hold organisations, watchdogs and chief executives to account. And not just teachers – even student and parental views can go viral within minutes, with a simple 'social share' of a poorly written, error-filled, home-school letter.

We can create and share petitions and see the impact our online voices can have on parliament and policy. The beginning of transparency and the (beginning of the) end to opaqueness is upon us and it is necessary that all educators consider congregating online to share and improve the work we do. However, with the rise of 'fake news' and sponsored content, how do we know what online content is genuine or fabricated?

Academic research from Rutgers University[8] examined the characteristics of social activity and patterns of communication on Twitter; a prominent example of the emerging class of communication systems that is called 'social awareness streams.' The research aimed to acquire an understanding of the type of content shared by individuals, with the main objective to identify different types of user activity, specifically focusing on message content and its relationship to patterns of use. Rutgers used content from over 350 Twitter users, applying coding and quantitative analysis to provide an understanding of the activity of individuals on the network. The analysis suggested two common types of user behaviour in terms of:

- the content of the posted messages
- exposed differences between users in respect to these activities.

---

[8] Naaman, M Boase, J & Chih-Hui L *Is it Really About Me? Message Content in Social Awareness Streams*, (2010)

Four dominant categories were provided in the analysis – Information Sharing (IS) – 22% of messages were coded in that category; Opinions and Complaints (OC), statements (RT) and "me now" (ME). The latter dominated the dataset (showing that, indeed, "it's all about me" for much of the time). As in education, Twitter users represent two different types of "content camps" – the majority of users focus on the "self" and a smaller set of users are driven more by sharing information. How similar is this to any education institution? Leaders focused on their priorities and projects, with teachers focused on sharing and classroom teaching.

Rutgers concluded that users benefit from social learning and are influenced by the activity of others they observe on the service. The findings suggested that users in the 'information sharing' group tend to be more conversational, posting mentions and replies to other users, and are more embedded in social interaction on Twitter, having more social contacts. One hypothesis is that informers (those who provide information that helps others) prove more "interesting", attract followers, and therefore make more use of Twitter's social functions. Another is that an increased amount of followers encourages users to post additional (informative) content. On the contrary, a me-informer, someone who simply looks to gain attention from little investment, shares 'status updates all about me'.

The Future

Out of the doldrums, every teacher can stand tall. We have a platform to share our voices; the rise of the socially connected teacher has given everyone a forum to share what was considered 'just a worksheet' or an idea dismissed by our line-managers. There are over 4,000 *unofficial* bloggers registered in the UK. The education community is still growing, with an estimated 5%-10% of the (1 million) education professionals using Twitter in England. The immediacy of social media means that we now expect instant feedback from policy makers and want to hold them to account.

We teach in schools to improve the lives of the children. We teach because we thrive through teaching students, and by creating resources for our classrooms. We train to empower the staff we work with, and help unlock their potential in the classroom. Yet, this would all be meaningless without relationships with our colleagues, whether physical or digital. With the social media era upon us, who knows what the next 20 or 50 years will look like for education. What will web 3.0 or web 4.0 look like?

Some suggest that the current model for our schools and examinations will soon become obsolete. Students will congregate online to learn and teachers will drive pedagogy. If teachers mobilise, they can shape policy and influence 'what works' in the classroom, rather than being shaped by ideological whims and preferences.

With hashtags now part and parcel of our everyday lives, socially-connected teachers are not just a teacher, they are now resource-shop owners, publishers, event managers and writers. Educational publications now quote teacher-bloggers regularly and my advice to teachers using social media is:

- Be authentic and define what you share and why you connect with others online
- Learn to share, often
- Interact with others over a period of time to establish online trust

- Master the tools. Understand how various platforms work and break through the pain barrier of learning how to use any software platform
- Observe online etiquette and use it to your advantage to develop professionally, as well as enhance the work you are doing in education
- Remember that not only is content king – nobody follows a dormant profile – manage content, moderate and update regularly
- Reply to conversations in a timely manner
- Ignore unsavoury discussions and subversion
- Use social media tools to your advantage and take control – not only of your professional development, but of your wellbeing and mental health. Use in moderation.

What teachers say online can be very different from what one would say in person. It can be easy to be consumed by blogs, tweets, surveys, publications and requests to 'read this', 'read that', 'share this' and 'retweet please'. It can also be daunting if you don't know how to take control – so that being socially connected doesn't become a 24/7 task. However, know this: the socially-connected teacher is networked to a web of hundreds of individuals – colleagues far beyond the school gates seeking ideas, support, new opportunities and reassurance. It would take a foolish politician and school leader to ignore them. My advice is get connected too, to better yourself and to help build a common sense, pragmatic, education system.

Ross Morrison McGill is one of the most followed educators on Twitter in the UK and founder of one of the most popular education websites in the UK. He is an experienced school leader and in 2015 was nominated by Debrett's as one of the '500 Most Influential People In Britain'.

CHAPTER 7

No Parent Left Behind
How parents can be an active resource for schools

by Claudia Barwell

When I was eighteen I intentionally tried to fail my public exams.

I did so for two reasons. It angered me that all my education and learning in a subject could be distilled down to a single grade. It didn't feel representative of the highs and lows of my education.

Secondly, my parents desperately wanted me to go to university and I desperately didn't want to go. I thought that if I failed my A Levels, they wouldn't have a choice, university wouldn't accept me and I could do what I liked. The school was designed to serve the selection needs of universities, not the needs of its students. I felt I was on a conveyor belt and I wanted to get off.

My parents wanted me to go to university because of their cultural norms. I don't think they had any ambition for me in terms of what I studied, or what I would go on to do. As a parent, if your child had made it through school and got into university – job done. They were just doing the same as everyone else.

Now I'm a parent. My daughter is in school and now the cultural pressures are upon me. Is she doing well enough? Is she being stretched enough? How can we help at home with maths as well as reading? What areas are more challenging for her? And, of course, there is no escaping the big one: how does she compare to the other kids in her class? How does she fare in tests?

I want to be able to play an active role in my daughter's learning at school so that I can support her at home. I want to feel like a critical part of her team, but in reality, I often feel intimidated by the school and redundant in her learning journey.

Aged five, my daughter comes home with language I don't recognise from my own education. Her's is a world of diagraphs and descenders, number bonds and chunking, phonemes and sound mats. Can I really help if I don't know my Kung Foo Maths from my Cuisenaire Rods?

My best example is when her reading journal came home with just the words "Orange Band". I wrote back complaining that without context, or even a recognisable book scheme, this meant nothing to me and I needed some guidance. The reply from her teacher was clear: "If you don't know what to do, try Googling it." In other words, I really haven't got the time to help you as well as the thirty kids in my class. I did Google "Orange Band" and discovered that it was an American pop/punk band from Los Angeles. Not very helpful and nothing to do with primary level literacy.

As parents, if we wish to change the global landscape of education, there are three things I believe to be fundamental: the teacher's relationship with parents, parents' relationship with formal assessment, and the latent power of parents in co-designing schooling.

Parents and Teachers

Teachers have a genuine challenge handling their relationship with parents. Striking the right balance in communication is complex when the parent demographic is so diverse. Schools who play to the lowest common denominator can end up patronising some parents using a level of language, literacy, and understanding they believe will alienate others. The requirement to differentiate between pupils in the classroom is transferred to their work with parents.

In that context, if you're a "parent", that is often all you are. I know teachers who are also parents who find the rigidity of that relationship particularly challenging. When they are in the role of "parent" they cannot be recognised as a fellow teacher too.

Whilst parents are almost universally self-taught, teachers are professionals. Their training covers the range of skills and competences they need. Some aspects of their role will consistently see them leading, particularly in teaching knowledge. They must be in charge in the classroom and create the right learning environment for their class.

The parent is typically the expert on their own child. This expertise can help the teacher become better in the behaviour management of individual children, which is then aggregated to a whole class. Similarly in role modelling, mentoring, child protection, and other core functions of being a teacher. Unpicking a teacher's responsibilities helps to develop a more differentiated relationship with parents.

On this basis, it seems possible for teachers and parents to have a valuable exchange, and create a relationship of mutual understanding. I think it would be helpful, for example, for teachers to receive a report from the parents about the child (not just the other way around). This could reflect the child's home life in the way that a school report reflects a child's school life and would particularly focus on behaviour, and on a child's motivation and passions. As more home-school communication is now delivered online, this could be achievable in real-time reporting.

Parents and Testing

When my aunt was fifteen, she came home from school one day and announced that she was dropping three subjects; French, History and Art. Furthermore, the private school she attended was supporting her decision. My grandfather was furious. In a meeting with the headteacher, it was explained that my Aunt would get better exam grades if she dropped these three subjects and concentrated on the others. It was unlikely she would get good grades in French, History and Art; she might not even pass. My grandfather was having none of it. He told them, "I'm not paying you to get my daughter to pass exams, I am paying you to educate her and that's exactly what I wish you to do."

In this anecdote I don't think my grandfather was particularly enlightened or forward-thinking, he was just using common sense. But it is also a reflection of the culture in schools that the outcomes that matter, above all others, are test scores. This has worsened as those exam results are now widely used for school accountability.

I know first-hand from teachers I have worked with that they often have a clear choice between educating or teaching a child to pass the test. They do not have the freedom or time to do both. Either learn to speak French so that you can hold a conversation, or get a good grade in the exam? In English, just study the chapter and the themes for the test, or read the whole book and discover a passion for reading?

The irony is that the currency of these tests, as a gateway to getting a job, is diminishing. More employers from Google to the UK Civil Service are screening for demonstrable skills over qualifications as a proxy for skill. My friend, who works as head of corporate PR for a FTSE 100 company, tells me that when recruiting, they have no interest in qualifications at all, they only look at experience. To be clear, applicants need education to be able to put together a CV and cover letter, (she throws anything with grammatical or spelling errors straight in the reject pile) but the English grades themselves are not important. The message from employers is becoming increasingly clear: "You need to do the work, but you don't need to ace the test."

Every parent's paradox is that they know that good grades only reflect one aspect of success at school, yet all they've got to value is what is easily measurable. Ken Robinson's "creativity", Angela Duckworth's "grit", Sugata Mitra's "curiosity" – they all resonate and we know they matter. These are things I believe to be at the core of a great education, but I don't believe we should be finding ways to measure them.

I also want my child to be continually developing as a person. That's my responsibility as a parent. But I need help from school. Together we can deliver this. I can support teachers in knowledge development, and they can help in developing my child's character, and other areas of personal development.

This vision of co-produced schooling needs a shift in paradigm. It needs a co-designed service.

Parents as Co-designers

What would this look like? Starting at school level, let's survey parents and ask some key questions.

What values do you believe are essential for a developing child?

What part of the current curriculum is essential?

What should we be teaching that we are not?

What skills will they need for the future?

What role would you like to play in the education of your children?

Posing these questions at scale would create a relationship based upon utilising parents as a resource. Include them in the design of education and then recruit their skills and talents to support the delivery. This progresses parents from a latent to an active resource.

Example: My child's school uses parents' and grandparents' knowledge on an ad hoc basis to support teachers in their instructional role. I recently visited a parent-promoted school in Canada that is active in engaging these resources by design, not by serendipity. What if time could be put aside for each class to have a workshop run by a volunteer parent? In my street we have parents who are animators, journalists, politicians, welfare dependents, architects, accountants, builders, theatre technicians, and chefs. They all have expertise to offer. What if that were expected in every school? I believe that even the busiest of parents would find the time – if only just once in their child's time in school – and many would be inspired by the opportunity to do more. Crucially, by design, it puts parents into the heart of the school community as active and engaged adults, a valuable resource for teaching and learning.

But in order to help with formal learning, parents would benefit greatly from an overview of what is being taught that year or term. Sharing teachers' planning could include links to teaching methods and a glossary of terms, so that we can support learning at home without being told we are "doing it wrong" by our children.

By being more familiar with their child's learning, parents would then have a much better understanding of how they're doing. Parents everywhere want reassurance that their child is flourishing, and are currently protective of formal testing, because it provides objective feedback. But those educators who would rather reallocate the time and money spent on (over) testing children, would find that parents become powerful allies once they have become more involved in the learning itself.

The prize is then a school that keeps dynamically re-aligning itself to the evolving values and views of its parent body. Teachers then have allies at home who can help with a range of responsibilities, and in return teachers gain an understanding of the individual child and how better to support them. The parent body becomes a group supporting each other, supporting teachers, who better support their children.

As an 18 year old, I didn't succeed in failing my public exams – I got a degree after all. I am not a teacher but I am an education professional. In my work, I bring together educators, policy makers, academics, and education business leaders to exchange ideas about school reform. I attend countless events that do the same. At the best events we listen to students. But in all education stakeholder conversations, parents are never included. We even leave our own experience as parents outside the discussion. No one has a more vested interest in the future of education than parents. Just imagine the potential we could unlock.

The original version of this essay was part of the Brookings Series: Meaningful Education in Times of Uncertainty

---

Claudia Barwell is director of learning at *Suklaa* and co-founder of *Oppi Festival*. Her work focuses on creativity, innovation and change-making in education. Often working in an international context, she organises learning events for teachers and young people. Suklaa's work is characterised by informality, crowdsourcing and empowering those within the education system.

MAKING IT COUNT

Examinations, Evidence and Outcomes

CHAPTER 8

Does it Count?
It's time to tell the emperor he's naked…

by David Price

Ask any teacher, anywhere in the world, what is the most frequently asked question they get asked by their students and they'll almost certainly reply, "Why do we have to learn this?" The teacher then responds with a mildly-exasperated sigh. Personally I had no problem during my fifteen-year teaching career with my students asking this. If they've given up over a third of their waking hours to be in your company I figure they deserve an answer.

However, the good news for exasperated teachers is that "Why do we have to learn this?" may now have been knocked off the top spot. The bad news is that its successor tends to provoke even more exasperation. When assigning tasks, today's teacher, in most developed countries, is now likely to be met with "Does it count?"

Loosely translated, this means "Are there marks for this coursework?", or "Is it going to be on the test, because if it's not, I'm not doing it." This isn't what most educators came into teaching for. But, once again, I don't think we can blame the students.

I was once in a bar in London. The young barman turned out to be a post-graduate, and I asked him what else he did to earn a living. "I write degree dissertations for Chinese students – five hundred pounds for five thousand words." Trying to stifle my holier-than-thou-ness, I mumbled, "Tell me, do you not feel, well, morally compromised by doing that?" His response was unforgettable. He shrugged, and said: "It's the end-result of a market-driven system."

And that's why we can't get too upset by our classroom students' question – they're merely the end-result of a market-driven system. As I write, the big news story on TV concerns the uncovering of the practice of excluding students at St Olave's Grammar School in South-East London (founded 1571), because their interim tests predicted they would fail to get a B, or above, in their A-level examinations. The school has since relented, but, according to the Times Educational Supplement, around twenty thousand students per year[9] quit before taking their terminal exams. It's impossible to say how many of them left voluntarily, or were pushed out, but you don't have to look very far to see the driving force behind the St Olave's exclusions. Their website homepage boasts:

> *"In a record year at St Olave's Grammar School, students achieved a stunning 96% A*/B grades. A total of 75% of all grades were at A*/A, 3 percentage points up on last year's. 32 students gained straight A* grades in at least 3 subjects. We did this by kicking out the dross that would have besmirched our reputation by getting a 'C' in their A-levels."*

---

[9] https://www.tes.com/news/school-news/breaking-news/more-20k-pupils-leave-school-sixth-forms-end-a-level-courses

OK, so I made that last sentence up. But whichever way you look at it, it's pretty reprehensible behaviour. However, the pressure placed on schools by the publication of school league tables is potentially corrupting – whether you are St Olave's, and *especially* if you are an inner-city high school, dealing with a host of social problems in a 'no-excuses' culture. Is it so surprising that some feel obliged to game the system?

Like the London barman who helped Chinese students buy their degrees, St Olave's and the rest are simply proving that W.E. Demming, the management guru, was right when he said "It's human nature – give me a target, and I'll find a way to hit it."

The frequently unasked question, however, burrowing at the heart of the 'Does it count?' dilemma is this: Does our apparent obsession with standardised testing count? Let's take a look at this from a number of perspectives:

Does it count towards improving our education system?

At first glance the answer to this question would be an obvious 'yes'. I mean, how else are we going to know if any given instructional strategy works, except by rigorously gathering evidence of its impact? The 'datafication of education' is rampant. While working in Australia, I was shown a report card for a student at a school in South-East England. It was simply a print-out of the mass of data collected on the student, including interim test scores, targets and predicted grades, for each subject studied. No comments. No data on the student's contribution to class discussions or wellbeing. Just a bunch of letters and numbers. The horrified Australian teacher was sharing it with colleagues as a warning that they could be heading down the same data-obsessed road.

Of course, data is important. It can inform changes of practice and policy. But a slavish adherence to data can be depersonalising, deskilling and destabilising for parents, teachers and students. But perhaps these are sacrifices worth making if the end goal is unambiguous proof of effective teaching practice?

In the US, UK and Australia, various versions of 'What Works' are being touted as the key to objective 'evidence-based improvement'. I'm not arguing that any skilled practitioner shouldn't be gathering data on their student's progress, but as we've already seen, when that evidence is gathered under high-stakes conditions, it can be subject to distortion. And when it's the only evidence gathered, as is the case in most educational trials, then things can get dangerously prescriptive. In the overwhelming majority of trials, evaluations and pilot initiatives, the sole yardstick is - did the student's test scores improve? This is an overly-narrow arbiter of success and, as has been pointed out by Prof. Yong Zhao and others, ignores the side-effects of any given intervention. We wouldn't approve a cancer treatment, however successful, if the patient suffered a total loss of appetite and subsequent starvation. So, why do we approve literacy interventions without checking to see if the side effects include, say, the student's desire to read?

Unless we want to regard kids as a set of automated widgets in a factory, shouldn't we be coming to conclusions on what works by drawing on a far wider set of indicators?

Does it count towards national prosperity?

Categorically not. The PISA international assessments of performance in Literacy, Numeracy and Science have become the holy grail of evidence, when in fact they are the Emperor's New Clothes of education. In fairness, the OECD, who administer the tests, never intended for them to be the triennial judgement on whether we're all going to hell in a handcart – it's just politicians and journalists that have turned them into the ultimate high-stakes test. National education strategies all over the world are formulated with the desired intent to 'make our nation globally competitive', invariably citing run-of-the-mill performances in PISA league tables as warning signs that, in the race-to-the-top, we are falling behind.

The ridiculous over-simplification of these pronouncements can be exposed by looking at just one country's correlation with PISA over a range of measures: America. Out of more than 65 countries assessed by PISA, the United States has consistently ranked mid-table. Could do better. Cue Secretaries of State for Education in the White House, over nearly 20 years, calling for more standardised testing to improve student performance (which is akin to growing healthy plants by pulling them up on a regular basis to see how they're doing). So, let's see how it's affecting their national performances:

- Institute for Management Development's Index of Global Competitiveness 1996-2015 #1: USA
- Thomson Reuters Analysis of Scientific Papers Published 2001-2011 #1: USA
- Number of Mathematics Papers published #1: USA
- Global Creativity Index 2015 #2: USA

- Innovation Index (as judged by patents produced) #1: USA
- Global Entrepreneurship Index #1: USA

(Note: the target populations for most of the above were adults aged 25 to 35. PISA performance of this age cohort during 2000-2009 – when they were 15 year-olds – for reading, maths and science, have been on, or close to, OECD mean scores. Mid-table obscurity, in other words).[10]

'PISA Hysteria' isn't based upon any sensible correlation between a country's ranking and a range of prosperity measures. So, why does it matter? Because the drive behind more standardised testing, across a range of countries, is fuelled, primarily, by official responses to PISA results. Roll on the day when an Education Secretary of State responds to PISA by saying "We've looked at the data and decided that it doesn't really tell us anything, so we'll keep doing what we think is best for the wellbeing and future prospects of our children." Maybe the Finns already did it. Here in the UK, if the education strategies of successive governments has been to significantly improve our performance in global rankings, then we have succeeded in making our kids miserable (as Madeleine Holt and John Rees will attest in the following chapters), but failed miserably in the government's stated objective. Lose-lose. Rather than accept that the 'exam factories' that our schools have become, doesn't work, for anyone, some government ministers and,

---

[10] http://christienken.com/2016/11/15/pisa-results-are-coming-and-why-it-does-not-matter

shamefully, some educators, blame the students, labelling them 'generation snowflake'[11].

Does it count for our children's life chances?

Apparently not. Despite its seemingly counter-intuitive nature, test scores do not indicate who's going to succeed in getting into university, or into well-paid employment. Research suggests a range of significantly better indicators: the obvious one of economic status; levels of self-belief; the ability to build relationships and networks; resilience...all better at predicting future success than how well they did in exams.

This collective self-delusion – that performance in academic tests predicts future success in life – is at the heart of what Guy Claxton described at the start of this book: swathes of children feeling inadequate as a result of the false elevation of the intellectual over the practical. The consequence of this denigration of vocational skills, from successive governments, couldn't be more ironic: the very jobs that are hard for machines to replace are of the 'non-routine manual' variety (electricians, plasterers, plumbers). Yet our current system is churning out students who can do 'routine cognitive' tasks (office admin workers who process information) that robots can do miles better than humans.

We all want our children to be secure later in life. So, what *does* indicate their future life chances? During the past couple of years a number of studies point to two highly correlated indicators: reading for pleasure and student

---

[11] Collins Dictionary defines it as a collective term for young adults of the 2010s

engagement. Numerous studies have linked the so-called 'reading quotient' (the amount of leisure reading a child is engaged in) with academic performance and career/college readiness[12]. Equally, a twenty year longitudinal study[13] found that children's interest and engagement in school influences their prospects of educational and occupational success 20 years later, *over and above their academic attainment and socioeconomic background.* In case you missed that, it found that exams were a poor proxy for kid's life chances, and that an engaged child from a low socio-economic group would fare better, twenty years on, than a disengaged child from a middle-class background.

In the context of seemingly ever-widening social inequality, doesn't it make sense to focus our energies upon the things that we currently *don't* measure but that clearly make a difference to kids' long-term future prospects, like reading for pleasure and being engaged in school?

Ah, but there's the rub – long-term. Everything about our education system has to be judged in the short-term. Education ministers get four to five years (if they're lucky) to make their mark and be judged accordingly; schools are judged by their ability to push their students one more rung up the ladder (high-school or college), and colleges are judged by short-term employability rates. How different would school's priorities look if they were judged by their student's life prospects 10, 15 or even 20 years after they left, rather than last year's exam results?

---

[12] See www.readkiddoread.com for a wide range of evidence

[13] Abbott-Chapman,J et al, *The longitudinal association of childhood school engagement with adult educational and occupational achievement: findings from an Australian national study* (2013) British Education Research Journal

Does it count for employers and colleges?

Currently, the only truthful answer is yes. Exam grades still open or close doors. But talk to any college admissions officer, or any head of human resources, and they'll tell you that it's a question of convenience, not preference. Faced with thousands of applicants, some filters have to be applied – but no-one is very happy with the current system of grade cut-off. That dissatisfaction is only going to grow, as the costs of making the wrong selections outweigh the convenience.

Some of the world's biggest corporations, including Google, Ernst & Young, Apple, Costco, IBM, are no longer interested in whether the applicant has a degree, arguing that it's not *what* you know that matters, but what you can *do* with what you know. So, the jobs of the future will increasingly ask for an applicant's portfolio, or their networks, or their LinkedIn recommendations, rather than a qualification. Companies like Entelo help companies like Cisco, Sony, Netflix, United Airlines and Tesla, overcome this dissatisfaction with the traditional CV/degree selection process, by using incredibly sophisticated software that 'mines every social network on the internet to identify hundreds of millions of potential candidates, then uses predictive analytics to identify the best fit according to criteria set by the client.

When the number of companies using big data, rather than student grades, to identify talent reaches a tipping point, then the whole edifice of standardised testing ceases to have relevance. Employers no longer rely on qualifications, so colleges and schools have to re-think assessment requirements. The ability to recall and regurgitate in a timed exam disappears – acquiring skills, learning dispositions and building a portfolio replaces test prep. Some visionary schools and universities already do this, but they're still the beautiful exceptions. In time, it will become the norm.

Does it count for schools and teachers?

Absolutely, with no imminent relaxation in high-stakes accountability on the horizon, it takes a brave school leader to speak out. One who did was Rachel Tomlinson, the headteacher of Barrowford Primary School in Lancashire, England. Writing to parents following their Standard Attainment Tests, Rachel praised the children's efforts, but made it clear that the school did not see their scores as representative of their true talents:

> *'We are concerned that these tests do not always assess all of what it is that make each of you special and unique. The people who create these tests and score them do not know each of you – the way your teachers do, the way I hope to, and certainly not the way your families do. They do not know that many of you speak two languages. They do not know that you can play a musical instrument or that you can dance or paint a picture.'*

The letter was picked up by Twitter and went viral. Rachel, astonished by the reaction, soon found out that public disagreement with 'what counts' has consequences. Within a year, the schools inspections agency OFSTED had visited the school, and judged it 'inadequate', commenting that *"The headteacher's leadership has emphasised developing pupils' emotional and social wellbeing more than the attainment of high standards."* Curiously, the school's previous inspection, in 2012, judged the school 'good' – the same conclusion as the most recent inspection, in 2016. Good in 2012. Good in 2016. Inadequate in 2015, the year after speaking out against high stakes testing. Coincidental?

Another leader that has tried to balance the development of future-focused skills with the need to achieve acceptable standardised test-scores, is Mark Moorhouse, headteacher of Matthew Moss High School (MMHS) in Rochdale, England. Serving a neighbourhood of high diversity and low socioeconomic status, the school has prioritised the development of self-directed learning skills. An independent report from the University of Bristol[14], on how their students fared beyond school, found that such a focus meant that MMHS students who went on to further study 'performed at a higher level than comparable cohorts of students from other schools', and that 'this capability stays with them in their onward destinations in formal education'. This commitment to students' long-term prospects gains no credit and shows up on no report cards. But schools like Matthew Moss do it anyway – because it's the right thing to do. And if the system could end its fixation with such a narrow set of measures, as Mark Moorhouse argues, we'd liberate our schools *and* our young people:

> *"It is entirely possible for schools to deliver academic excellence within a developmental experience which equips young people to thrive in the shifting world of the 21st century. And with a green light from those in*

---

[14] Crick, Huang, Munoz & Small *Freedom to learn and engage: the impact of a learner-centred pedagogy on student progress, outcomes and prospects* (2014) University of Bristol

power, they would, producing huge social, economic and personal benefit."

With more UK teachers leaving the profession than joining it, there's an urgent need to ask why it's become such an undesirable occupation. A Guardian survey last year found that 43% of teachers in England's state schools were planning on leaving within the next five years. So, a crisis looms. When asked why they're leaving, teachers almost always cite workload as the primary reason. But it's not simply the amount of work. It's what they see as the pointlessness of the data-collection, target setting, form-filling. All of it created to ensure that OFSTED inspections are passed, evidence can be produced, results can be defended, and students can be adequately prepared for tests that increasingly meet no needs, other than politicians needing to 'make schools accountable'.

Zoe Brown, one of those who left the profession in 2016, told *The Independent* newspaper: *"In some ways I don't feel like a teacher at all anymore. I prepare children for tests and, if I'm honest, I do it quite well. It's not something I'm particularly proud of, as it's not as if I have provided my class with any transferable, real-life skills during the process. They've not enjoyed it, I've not enjoyed it, but we've done it: one thing my children know how to do is answer test questions."*

Does it count towards a future-ready society?

The point of intense frustration for many is that it doesn't have to be like this. As we've seen, technology now enables employers to harness the incredible power and sophistication of social and predictive analytics to hire just the right employee, instead of the one with the best grades, or resume. Those same technologies could be used by schools to provide a complete, individualised picture of a student's growth – academic, vocational, creative, personal and social, among many other datasets – instead of pigeonholing them by their grades. In no way should this make schools any less accountable. Indeed, their accountability could only widen as a broader range of stakeholders have a profile of the student's progress. Parents, potential employers, college admissions staff and not least students themselves, would all have the information they need to have rich conversations about students' unique talents, their ability to work in teams, what they've made and the networks they've built, their resilience when handling setbacks, their commitment to learning outside, and beyond, school – and their capacity, as Valerie Hannon said earlier, to *thrive*.

Some of the following essays will argue that the impact of testing is damaging to the wellbeing and mental health of our children. I've tried to argue that *what* we're measuring increasingly counts for less and less. That it tells us next-to-nothing about: what employers are looking for; where students' talents lie; their long-term prospects; how effective schools are in growing them as engaged, culturally aware citizens; our national prosperity, and their readiness for the workplace, or further study. The high stakes accountability attached to what we're measuring is a corrosive, corrupting force that is 'de-moral-ising' too many educators into gaming the system, simply to survive.

Yet still we persist. The emperor has no clothes, and it's time someone told him. Does it count? You bet it does.

David Price is an author, speaker, consultant and trainer. He specialises in helping organisations – schools, colleges, as well as commercial organisations – prepare for a complex future. His book, *OPEN: How We'll Work, Live and Learn in the Future* has been an Amazon bestseller since its publication in 2013. In 2009 he was awarded the O.B.E. by Her Majesty the Queen, for services to education. He works in several countries, mainly the UK, Australia, USA and Europe, training teachers, working strategically with education departments, and speaking at international conferences. He is a board member for the Canadian Educators Association, and VEGA Schools in India.

CHAPTER 9

Leaders Owning
what Matters

by Liz Robinson

As a school leader, it is easy to feel brow-beaten by the combination of seemingly constant change combined with high stakes accountability. For over a decade, I have been head of a primary school serving a challenged community in South East London, and I have learned the critical importance of finding a core confidence in my vision and values, as a way to ensure we are able to run the school as we believe we should. I have led four Ofsted inspections as head, each under significantly different frameworks and expectations. As such, I have deeply experienced these challenges first hand.

What has perhaps influenced my views most deeply in this period has been becoming a mother myself. This highly personal take on the purpose of education (balance of knowledge, skills, competency, socialisation and exam performance) gives me a visceral experience on what school could or should be.

Education remains a highly political sphere in the UK. This means priorities shift frequently; and so too does the apparatus for measuring the efficacy of schools in delivering those outcomes. In fact, my experience is that the latter (Ofsted, league tables, regional school commissioner teams) have become so dominant, that the debate about the core purpose is often a sorry after-thought.

Given the critical importance of our work, and our status as publicly funded institutions, scrutiny and public accountability are to be expected and welcomed.

However, the challenge for schools is that the views about what it means to have done a good job vary hugely (e.g. test scores, communication skills, active citizenship), both between stakeholders, and, critically, over time. This flux and variation, has eroded the capacity and confidence of school leaders to shape and define their own vision, and really do what they believe to be right.

As a result, too many schools simply now do what they know Ofsted will be looking for, and/or what delivers results in the narrow band of academic outcomes being measured. When speaking to other heads, or aspiring leaders, I ask them about their strategic vision for their schools. Ofsted usually comes out as the first response. Although understandable, I find this worrying and depressing.

Internally referenced vision – owning what matters

Those who are heavily 'externally' referenced lack confidence in themselves, needing the views of others to reinforce, support or challenge. Conversely, 'internally' referenced individuals have the confidence to act with autonomy, to trust themselves and their own ideas and hold their own view about who they are and are not. This does not mean ignoring the expectations of others, or being inward looking; it must be responsible and based on evidence and experience. It is not a whim, and not an ideology.

It is time for more school leaders to develop such a vision. We must;

- Be disciplined in understanding the needs of those we serve
- Do all we can to meet those needs
- Know that part of our role must also be to demonstrate the effectiveness of our approaches to all our stakeholders

This is highly challenging for school leaders to develop and sustain, given the potentially career-ending nature of external scrutiny. But, it is also critical if we are to develop the kinds of schools, and the kinds of leaders who will run them, that we so need. We need to find the confidence, courage and humility to be true leaders.

Having worked with inspirational staff, pupils and parents, I am immensely proud of the vision we have created – one which now underpins our highly successful school.

Our mission at Surrey Square

'Personal and academic excellence; everyone, every day.' These are the words we use to drive everything we do. We believe that a strong academic core is a necessary but not sufficient outcome for our pupils, and so the 'and' is key as it demonstrates our absolute commitment to excellence in both spheres of development. For us, 'personal excellence' is defined by our seven core values (respect, enjoyment, compassion, responsibility, perseverance, community and excellence); behaving and embodying these is our aim. To demonstrate each of those values in the way you conduct yourself is to show personal excellence, as is the ability to use the values as a tool for reflection, correction and learning when things go wrong.

'Everyone, every day' expresses deeply held beliefs about equity (we are all bound by these expectations; parents, leaders, governors) and in integrity (this is about doing it every day, not just for show). We also use this to surface that fact that 'every day' is really hard; creating and sustaining this excellence is really, really hard work, sustained over years.

So excellence needs balance, and, critically, our core values come as a set. Thus we must show compassion for each other when life is tough, demonstrate perseverance when we know we could have done better, and enjoyment when we are able to experience life's joys together.

Taking control – measuring success, our way

We adopt three approaches to drive own internally referenced vision, at pupil, school and inter-institutional level.

Pupil level accountability: measuring personal excellence

Many, if not all, schools, acknowledge the need to develop personal skills in their pupils. However, very few set about teaching, and assessing these skills with any kind of deep rigour. There are understandable reasons for this, given that we do not have anything close to an agreed framework in this area. However, if we are really committed to our 'internally referenced' vision that this matters, surely we should be finding ways to do this, with something approaching the consistency and effort we afford to academic performance.

Our approach has been;

- To timetable weekly teaching sessions
- To establish planning formats, resources and expectations
- To establish a progressive scale of skills for each value, and produce an attractive assessment record for every pupil
- To establish pupil level progress tracking for early identification of concerns and intervention planning

The effect of working in this way has been truly profound; the teaching of personal excellence is understood to be important and valued; teachers, parents and children experience the fact that our mission is not just words, but that we actively demonstrate our commitment to what we believe. Staff are proud to articulate and share the progress that children make, and are quicker to identify specific areas of need.

School level accountability; 'flipped quality assurance'

Despite every moment of externally imposed accountability that school leaders may experience, the most shocking thing for me is the extraordinary extent to which may of us go on to create exactly those same conditions within our institutions, through 'top-down' processes of internal accountability, usually known as 'monitoring'. Even Ofsted give you the opportunity to evaluate your own performance, before working with you to establish the accuracy of those judgements.

I had felt uncomfortable about our approach to monitoring for a number of years, seeing the amount of time and energy which was lost on 'playing a game',

My Perseverance Journey

	Year 1	Year 2...
I will give it a go with the support of someone I trust		
I can ask for help		
I can say why something is hard		
I can come up with possible solutions		
I can ask for specific help		
I will give it a go independently		
I accept that I will make 'juicy mistakes'		
I can listen to feedback		
I can learn from my juicy mistakes (I understand failure is important)		
I recognise the feelings that come with 'giving it a go'		
I make positive choices about my feelings when I am giving it a go		
I can celebrate mini successes		
I recognise when others find it hard to persevere / give it a go		
I can support others to persevere		
I am an ambassador for perseverance		
I can lead others in their perseverance journey		

however much we had tried to move away from high stakes observations.

This was brought to a head when I, and my co-head were on maternity leave (yes, both at the same time, terrible family planning!). They say the mark of a great leader is that they can walk away, and no one will notice. Well, suffice to say that it was a humbling experience for us both. Upon our return, we were disappointed in the lack of pride that effective practitioners were taking, the lack of leadership that effective leaders had demonstrated. Our long hard reflection was that, somehow, we had retained a role as the 'custodians of excellence' at the school. In our absence, no one else felt the same intensity, confidence or clarity to advocate for excellence.

We re-visited our mission, and 'everyone, every day' was born. For the last 5 years, we have revisited every process and system to support every single member of the school community to become a 'custodian of excellence'. Looking again at our approach to monitoring has been key.

What became very clear is that, despite softening the edges, the monitoring was still fundamentally based on a few of us (senior leaders) making judgements about the practice of everyone else.

We went back to the drawing board, and thought again what we really wanted to achieve with our approach. This was:

- Accurate understanding of daily practice across the school, in order to inform professional learning, staffing and support priorities

- Greater pride, motivation and commitment from all staff in doing their best all the time (personal and academic excellence; everyone, every day)
- Greater honesty and openness between staff and leaders about development needs
- Greater confidence in staff to articulate where they are being really successful and have practice to share
- More effective processes to reduce workload for all staff

Through this thinking we totally re-designed our approach, abandoning top down monitoring and creating a bottom up self-evaluating quality assurance model. Instead of a small group of leaders at the top of the organisation making judgements about the work of everyone else, we have found a way for teachers to take responsibility for their own practice, explicitly linking their own learning to their understanding of where their practice needs development.

The flip for us was to shift the assessment of this from the leaders to the individual teachers themselves. Simple self-assessment formats are the basis for a meeting, giving an opportunity for the teachers to show other colleagues evidence to support their own judgement.

Through working in this way, we have seen a marked change in both the efficacy and effect of quality assurance. We find that teachers are now highly attuned to their own practice, and make very accurate assessments of their own strengths (which is a skill in itself) as well as the things they need to work on. The changes have resulted in:

- Teachers feeling more respected and less scrutinised;
- Teachers being in the driving seat of their own professional learning;

- Teachers and leaders have saved time, and reduced workload;
- Leaders have finely tuned 'live' information about the practice across the school.

It is a simple but profound shift; to empower and enable teachers to tell leaders about their practice, rather than vice versa. Given the push to support pupils to take greater responsibility for their learning and assessment, it seems only right that we push for ways for this to be a reality for the teachers too.

Inter-Institutional Level – Peer Review

My interest in peer review comes from a profoundly upsetting experience of a dear friend and colleague head stepping down from her role following an inspection. Despite being close friends, I was struck by the fact that we had never really had the fundamental conversations about our schools that I had had with other colleagues. The top-down accountability approach takes away the likelihood and even legitimacy of such a conversation happening, even between close friends. We can become so reliant on other people telling us about our schools, we fail to discuss this with our peers and colleagues.

As a result, I was looking for a way to work differently with colleagues; a way of giving permission to have the big conversations in a way that works for everyone, and found this in the form of a peer review process designed by Education Development Trust.

Working in groups of 3-8 schools, leaders take it in turns to receive, lead and support reviews in one another's schools. The lead reviewer works with the host school to identify an area of focus, as well as a methodology for the review (what will the reviewers do/see on the day). A team of reviewers from various schools then conduct the review, and feedback to the host school at the end of the day.

A critical part of the process is a follow up workshop, which takes place about a week later. In some respects, the most skillful part of the work, a facilitator guides relevant staff from the host school through an 'improvement workshop', to unpick the issues and identify future actions.

We are now supporting a group of 24 schools in this process and have found the key positive impacts to be:

- Building of relationships – moving beyond 'polite' to deeper, trusting, professional dialogues
- Development opportunities for all involved
- Deep dives into aspects of practice with which schools have felt 'stuck' – time to focus on own agenda and get to the bottom of things
- Greater feeling of empowerment for leaders, feeling more in control of their school improvement, rather than being 'told' what to do

From my perspective, the difference it has made at a local level has been extraordinary, and exactly what is needed to put school leaders genuinely in a position to lead again. It is a structural shift which moves the conversation about your school from being 'one to which I am subject', to one in which I, as a head, am an equal partner.

Conclusion

'In education, we tend to turn out conformists, stereotypes, individuals whose education is completed, rather than freely creative and original thinkers... Why be concerned over this? In a time when knowledge,

constructive and destructive, is advancing by the most incredible leaps and bounds... unless individuals, groups and nations can imagine, construct, and creatively revise new ways of relating to these complex challenges, the lights will go out.'

– Carl Rogers[15]

Rogers wrote these words in 1961. I think they stand as a fantastic call to action for the leaders of our school system today. As heads, as leaders, we must find ways to embody what we really believe to be right and true, resist the (natural) tendency to conform, and start by making sure that the way we treat those in our schools is how we ourselves want to be treated. We must keep learning at the heart of what we do – learning for adults as well as children, creating environments where it is safe to share openly, to collaborate and learn from one another.

It is so important now for education leaders to create principled, thoughtful and effective approaches, which ensure that accountability and quality assurance are serving the right purpose; namely to ensure that every child in every school, regardless of background or circumstance, has access to an education which nurtures their potential, enabling them to thrive in the coming century.

Liz Robinson has led, and now co-leads, Surrey Square Primary School in Southwark. The school, located in an area of extreme social challenge, uses values as the vehicle to deliver 'personal and academic excellence', explicitly teaching and assessing a broad range of outcomes. Liz is passionate about developing

---

[15] *On becoming a person – A therapist's view of psychotherapy* (2014) Rogers, C. Robinson Publishing

leaders and she is the consultant director for Primary with *Future Leaders*. She is proud mummy to two young girls, and actively supports women and mothers in senior leadership roles in education.

CHAPTER 10

More Than a Score
Children are more than a set of data

by Madeleine Holt

Many parents don't know much about the sausage factory in which their children are being processed. But they do know that they are coming home bored and increasingly stressed. One report after another suggests that child mental health problems are rising. It's time to challenge the thinking behind the current barren vision for education. We need to tell parents and politicians that it doesn't have to be this way.

England is an international outlier in its obsession with standardised, high stakes tests. What sets us apart is linking students' scores with how schools are judged under a punitive inspection system. The story we've been sold for the last twenty five years is that only a system of rigid, test-based accountability will ensure that standards go up. The good news is that some brave schools in England are striking out, developing their own more revealing and effective ways of assessing children's learning. The result is an education that is both more humanist and more humane.

Some may think humane is a strong word to use, but I use it quite deliberately. There have been some specific changes made in primaries in the last couple of years, which could only be described as unkind. The Statutory Assessment Tests (SATs) which children have to take at the age of eleven are now pass or fail. Thanks to the former education secretary, Michael Gove, the tests have deliberately been made far harder. And yet there is absolutely no evidence from academics that children will rise to the challenge of tests that are inappropriate for their age.

So what is the result? In 2016, 47 per cent of all eleven-year-olds failed the SATs and were told they were "not secondary school ready". This year, 2017, many schools upped their game and engaged in turbocharged teaching to the test. Yet still 39 per cent of eleven-year-olds failed. In July their parents had to break the bad news to them. Then what happened? Children had six weeks to mull over this unjust decision. Many wondered if they would be put in the bottom set at secondary school or if they'd even be refused a place, never mind if they would ever succeed in getting a good job.

This is the importance children now attach to SATs results – I know this because I have interviewed them about it. Here's what some Year 6 children from two schools in the Midlands and North of England told me:

"SATS are to help us for our future and what we want to be."

"I get stressed in SATs and I worry if I won't get a good job or something. I know the stuff in the tests but sometimes I forget how to do it or I just make a little mistake and it'll affect the answer... If you want to be a writer you

can't really get a writer's job because you won't know the proper punctuations." (sic)

"I don't think we should do SATs because I don't really like seeing my friends sad and I don't like being sad myself."

Both schools are in areas of high deprivation. Staff have to accept that many of their children will fail the tests. As one teacher put it:

"I know for a fact that there will be a good percentage in my classroom that will be classed as a failure. They have got to go home and tell people at home that they have been deemed a failure. I just find it shocking... I think it's affecting their learning massively. I think they must be sat there day in day out having to listen to me teach things that don't mean anything to them. Their self-esteem must be sometimes on the floor."

Colin Harris, a former primary head and columnist for the Times Educational Supplement, vividly recalls SATs week at his school:

"I had a lot of children crying. I've had children running out of the building and we have had to go and get them. These children, when they were going into the playground, were trying to convince others not to do it anymore because it's not fair. The majority of schools have had to lie to children: we are trying to convince them of a system that is inherently wrong."

In fact, supposedly 'failing' pupils still go to their original secondary school, but they receive no statutory help or specialised teaching to boost their confidence. Even worse, many schools retest using their own assessments, because they don't trust the SATs results. It would be difficult to dream up a more effective system for making so many primary school children feel like abject failures for no good reason. So why are we doing it? Because government thinks that collecting test results from all children is the best way of judging and comparing the work of schools. Poor results can push schools down the league tables, sometimes to the point that headteachers are forced out and the school is removed from local authority control. In this way, children become caught up in a school improvement vision that's become heavily politicised. It's a toxic situation.

As for the pupils that do pass these questionable tests, what does a good score tell you? Most likely the school has taught to the test and/or the intake is likely to be more middle class, and as such the school has benefitted from the home support higher social status often brings. Does this mean that higher scores have ensured a higher standard of education, as ministers like to claim? Our current system guarantees this is the last thing we get. Instead, external tests are being used to control teachers and dictate the curriculum to the detriment of students

Add into the mix:

- the introduction of the spelling, punctuation and grammar test with its now infamous 'fronted adverbials', condemned by experts as serving no valid educational purpose
- the phonics check on five year olds, which research has shown does nothing to help children understand the meaning of words
- plans to revive a standardised "baseline" test on four year olds, some of whom will be less than 1,500 days old

Now you get an idea of the exhausting pressures faced by teachers, children and increasingly parents in English primary schools.

This is where More than a Score comes in. It's a new campaign to stop children being seen as little more than numbers. We are an alliance of parents and professionals inspired by the many alternatives to the high stakes testing which is preventing children from being themselves. It was born of frustration among teachers, academics and experts in mental health that the evidence they produced was until very recently steadfastly ignored by politicians. Could parents – the one group least likely to be ignored by politicians – feel frustrated enough to take out their resentment at the ballot box? At the last count there were 13.8 million households in England with dependent children. That's a lot of voters. Now was the time to get parents properly on board with an alliance for an alternative vision for primary education.

Parents were already getting organised among themselves. In a development not seen since protests against grammar schools in the 50s and 60s, they were setting up their own campaign groups. Let Our Kids be Kids took off on social media in just six weeks and staged the first ever children's strike against SATs. Their supporters deplored the fact that school days are now routinely focused on maths and English all morning – in preparation for SATs – while all other subjects and creative opportunities are squeezed into the margins of the curriculum. Meanwhile, Rescue Our Schools, which I co-founded, had a broad remit to challenge dogma-driven education policy. Both groups were happy to become part of something bigger which gave primary school parents something to believe in.

More than a Score officially launched in November last year and held its first conference in London in December. Since then there have been regional conferences in Newcastle, York and Oxford and grassroots groups have been set up by parents across England. There are now sixteen members of the coalition, among them BERA (the British Educational Research Association), the Association of Educational Psychologists and Slow Education. In March we launched our proposals for a new assessment framework that improves – not damages – primary education. None of us is against assessment or even testing. Our goal is to ensure it helps learning rather than hinders it.

Our vision is for assessment that:

- treats young people in the round, valuing a range of skills and attributes across the curriculum
- is appropriate to their development
- enables a dialogue between teachers and parents
- identifies schools that need extra support and develops improvement strategies in line with their values
- informs national standards of attainment across the whole curriculum

In practise this means trusting teachers (shock horror!) to use their professional expertise to deliver these goals. No one test can reasonably do this. We need different forms of assessment for different purposes. We would like to see teachers using what is known as formative and summative assessment. The first is ongoing and supports pupils while they are learning, based upon observing what they can do, and upon discussion and feedback between teacher and learner. It's standard practice in many jurisdictions, among them Scotland and Wales. Summative assessment – like SATs – tests pupils on what they have learnt at a particular point. Instead of testing students after a number of years, it could be used much more precisely – for example, at the end of a project, or unit of work.

A system of moderation by teachers between schools and a supportive school inspection framework would ensure staff could compare the progress of their pupils against national standards. Likewise, detailed reports of pupils' progress would be far more meaningful than a set of scores. The current Early Years Foundation Stage Profile used in English primaries is an excellent example of an approach that could be used to track children's learning throughout school. Prospective parents keen to choose the right school for their child would surely find anonymised, detailed reports on children's progress far more insightful than decontextualised figures in a school league table.

There is still clearly a need to monitor the standards of primary education, so we would propose using the sampling methods adopted in Scotland and New Zealand, for example. Sampling involves a small number of children randomly selected across schools and uses tests for which they cannot prepare. These tests can include different curriculum areas so that a picture of standards across the whole curriculum would become available, informing teachers' work. This method is already used by the Department for Education for evaluating standards in primary science.

Colin Harris believes if you get the curriculum right, the appropriate approach to assessment will follow. "It's got to be about creating first a curriculum that is acceptable to our children – that they are excited about. If schools have a set of parameters for a curriculum which the government lay out, I have no problem with that. That would enable schools to submit a curriculum utilising the resources around them – so if you've got space you could do an outdoor curriculum or whatever. And then you set an assessment package that is externally moderated. If we want our children to be individuals, you've got to create a package of assessment that is individual."

Even within the current system, many teachers are working on practical alternatives to the testing culture. Bealings is a tiny village school with a special needs intake of 25 per cent. Under its head, Duncan Bathgate, it has evolved a highly imaginative curriculum influenced by the Mantle of the Expert approach first developed by Dorothy Heathcote. Children take on expert roles within an imaginary team project inspired by real life.

When I arrived to film the school they were running a detective agency trying to solve various local legends. As I entered the classroom, I could see instantly that every young face was alert and engaged. Compare this with seeing rows of bored kids sitting at desks scribbling down facts about Greek myths. Out of their projects the Bealings students develop strong skills in communication, teamwork and problem solving and rich portfolios of work which can be shared with parents as evidence of their individual progress.

To meet the demands of the national curriculum Bealings' staff make detailed notes on every child, to ensure that through their various projects they are reaching statutory goals. But the notes serve a wider purpose as the school's own method of tracking progress. There is a rich irony that Bealings is regularly in the top 5 per cent of schools nationally for its SATs results and has had five

Outstanding OFSTED verdicts despite doing minimal preparation for standardised tests compared with most other schools.

Meanwhile in Oxford, at St Ebbe's school – a large primary with a mixed intake – staff have been experimenting with new ways of assessing maths. Year 5 has spent a year 'journaling' their work. They were encouraged to express their mathematical reasoning – something that SATs testing discourages – by regularly annotating their work with explanations of their thinking. On a number of occasions the method uncovered key misconceptions that would have gone undiscovered based on their answers and workings alone. The teachers involved found it was an invaluable tool in assessing maths through observation on an ongoing basis, counteracting the weaknesses of an assessment system based on standardised testing.

We know that other schools are finding space to challenge the test-driven regime. Some are doing it below the radar, others more publicly. The most resolute perhaps was the decision made in May 2017 by Jill Wood, the head of Little London community primary school in Leeds: her Year 6 students simply didn't sit SATs. The head teacher made her mind up the previous year after seeing the distress of her students as they prepared for and sat the newly difficult tests. The situation at Little London was particularly tough because of the high numbers of children who have English as their second language and the severe levels of poverty in the area.

Headteachers in England have a legal responsibility to put their ten and eleven year olds in for SATs. Jill Wood prepared carefully, winning over her staff, governors and parents. She informed the local authority that her students would not be doing them. The head made it clear that this was not a rejection of assessment: the school had been busy developing and strengthening an alternative approach. The Standards and Testing Agency was sent teacher assessments for Year 6 which had been carefully moderated by experienced teachers from three other local schools rated as Outstanding by OFSTED. They were informed that this would provide a far richer evaluation of children's achievements.

Little London is rigorous in its tracking of pupils' progress. Its marking policy is based on 'Assessment for Learning' principles, with teachers working with students on individual goals through constant feedback. Pupils are tested throughout the year to ensure they have mastered key knowledge in maths. And the rejection of test-driven hothousing has enabled the school to sustain a rich curriculum. Students' writing is not sacrificed to endless shoehorning of semicolons to meet Department for Education criteria.

SATs week came. The local education authority tried to visit, only to discover that Year 6 was away on an educational visit to Whitby. Since then the school's governors have stuck by their head, arguing that true leadership means putting children first. Judging by hundreds of supportive messages, it will be difficult for the powers that be to respond punitively.

Wood has no plans to lead a revolution, but perhaps that will happen in its own time. Much depends on whether key teacher unions will pursue an England-wide boycott. If not, there are signs parents will take things into their own hands. Already some are saying publicly that they will not put their children in for Year 6 SATS in May 2018.

After twenty five years of testmania, this particular chapter in the saga of English state education may be coming to an end. There are positive signs from many quarters. In May 2017 the all-party commons select committee of MPs on education reported that "many of the negative effects of assessment in primary schools are caused by the use of results in the accountability system. The government should act to lower the stakes and help teachers to deliver a broad, balanced and fulfilling curriculum."

At the same time a report commissioned by Pearson, the global business that administers SATs, concluded that teachers, parents, governors and pupils all feel anxiety over the impact of high stakes tests, and that the concerns of government are prioritised over and above the needs of teachers and pupils.

Meanwhile, the international momentum inclines towards a more sophisticated way of judging schools and standards. As Lucy Crehan concludes in her book *Cleverlands: The Secrets Behind the Success of the World's Education Superpowers*, using school-level data and irregular national assessments in supportive settings is a better way to build a high quality education system. A shared trait of all the countries she visited – Finland, Canada, Japan, China and Singapore – was a high level of professional autonomy for teachers. Most significantly, in the last few years the three Asian jurisdictions have all adjusted their curricula to encourage students to think outside the box. As if this weren't evidence enough, the OECD's 2013 analysis of effective assessment (based on a study of 28 countries) concluded that its fundamental purpose should be to improve student learning. To that end, it should have a broad scope so as to include critical thinking, social competences and overall wellbeing; it should be based on evidence; and it should try to build consensus among all stakeholders. Prophetically, it warns that if teachers are judged largely on the results of standardised tests, they may "teach to the test", giving less attention to students' wider educational and developmental needs.

Back in England, our approach has echoes of Victorian times as our primaries become little more than factories for producing the best possible SATs scores. Every day, every year, a test-driven curriculum is making it harder for children to become creative, critical thinkers – yet these are the very qualities they will need for the future. Our system cherishes numbers more than children. As a consequence we are harming thousands of young lives. It's time to stop the damage.

Madeleine Holt is an education campaigner. She helped set up *More than a Score*, an alliance of 17 organisations advocating alternatives to SATs and other standardised tests in English primary schools. Its members include BERA (the British Educational Research Association), the National Association of Educational Psychologists, Slow Education and Rescue Our Schools – a parent-led campaign group Madeleine co-founded to challenge dogma-driven education policy. She runs the social enterprise *Meet the Parents*, which encourages all families to consider sending their children to their local comprehensive. She was previously culture correspondent on Newsnight in a 20 year career at the BBC.

CHAPTER 11

Wellbeing and School Improvement

by John Rees

Looking back …

I remember it well. The 'Every Child Matters' agenda in the UK, supported by Public Health teams, was being promoted in every school in the country, and scrutinised by the schools inspection service, Ofsted. The National Healthy Schools programme was producing strong evidence of the links between pupils' wellbeing and their academic attainment. There was also a Government-funded training programme for teachers, school nurses, police officers and Youth workers to equip them to work together to provide Personal, Social, Health and Economic (PSHE) Education.

In 2008, to great acclaim, the Schools Minister announced that PSHE was to become a statutory part of the National Curriculum for state-funded schools in England. What could go wrong?

Within a matter of months, a general election had been called and the bill for statutory PSHE was lost in the 'wash up'. Government funding for the National Healthy Schools and PSHE Continuing Professional Development programmes was cut and the outcomes of 'Every Child Matters' was dropped from the lexicon of the Department for Education.

Five years later, Ofsted reported that the quality of PSHE education 'required improvement' or was inadequate in 40% of schools in England. Where PSHE was weaker, homophobic and disablist language was commonplace. Pupils' personal and social skills were weak – pupils had gaps in their knowledge, especially in relation to personal safety, mental health, and alcohol misuse. The same report lamented that those schools failing to provide high quality, age-appropriate sex and relationships education, could leave young people vulnerable to sexual exploitation.

Where are we now?

It's a sad indictment of education in the UK, especially England, that we have narrowed the success indicators for schools and individuals to a few things that we think we can measure. How many teachers joined the profession to teach children made-up words, such as in the phonics tests that all 7 year-olds must now take, and re-take when they are told that they are not good enough? How many teachers are happy to see their pay, promotion and even their livelihood at risk if children fail to reach a specific grade in English or Maths?

Of course, English and Maths are important. Basic levels of numeracy are essential to manage daily life and Mathematics forms the basis of so many careers in technology and engineering. Illiterate children cannot access the curriculum and are denied the pleasures of reading some of the greatest prose ever written. Although many will take issue with the assertions of Mr Gove, a recent Education Minister, that the joys of reading poetry would avert teenage pregnancies. But if we only teach those things that we can measure, are we in danger of only valuing that which we can assess?

Measuring children's problem-solving skills, their ability to work in groups, and their empathy to sensitively respond to the needs of others, are all essential skills that are needed by employers and society – but few schools find time to teach them, and fewer still find them easy to assess.

One in ten children have a diagnosable mental health problem. A recent survey suggested that 84% of UK teachers have suffered from mental health problems at some point over the last two years. In 2017, the Children's Commissioner for England reported that 580,000 young people – that's roughly equivalent to a city of the size of Manchester – are receiving some form of social care or assistance with mental health problems.

So, how can we reduce the suffering of teachers and pupils from mental health problems? Part of the answer lies in changing the balance of the curriculum and how we test, assess and report pupil's learning. It is a strange paradox that in theory many of the things that should promote wellbeing are often in place, but schools in England are saddled with a knowledge-based curriculum, tested in ways that create 'league tables', that increases pressure on schools and their staff. The outcome of such pressures frequently prevents schools from promoting health and wellbeing of children and staff.

Despite strong evidence of the links between pupil wellbeing and their attainment, PSHE is still not compulsory (more of this later). Research suggests that as much as 8% of the variation in pupil attainment could be attributed to teacher wellbeing. Staff wellbeing is therefore an important component of promoting pupils' achievement.

Let's start with what children need. Many children currently in primary schools, are likely to live into the 22nd

century. What we know of their future is that we know very little. They will have to deal with climate change, mass migration and increasing automation, but they will also have to manage challenges that we have not yet imagined.

Given the exponential changes in the ease of personal and global communication, there is a strong argument that a knowledge-based curriculum is unlikely to meet the future, or even current, needs of children. If I forget the capital of Alaska or a specific method of calculus, I can check it out on a personal communication device in a matter of moments. This challenges those schools who seek to ban the use of mobile phones. The majority of children over the age of ten will have easy access to a communication device which, in many schools, they are not allowed to use for learning. Misuse of mobile technology is surely a matter of behaviour management, not a reason to prohibit its use.

A values-based curriculum, that promotes pupils' spiritual, social, cultural and moral (SMSC) development, supported by specific teaching in PSHE education, can help improve both learning and wellbeing. For clarity, PSHE education may be described as timetabled lessons, whereas SMSC is something that happens throughout the curriculum, and extracurricular activities, the whole ethos of the school.

It has long been recognised that children's SMSC development underpins learning. In the UK, the 1944 'Education Act' gave Local Education Authorities the duty to contribute towards *the spiritual, moral, mental, and physical development of the community*. The importance of SMSC is still recognised as all state-funded schools are required to meet the National Curriculum expectations to:

'... make provision for personal, social, health and economic education (PSHE), drawing on good practice' and must offer a curriculum which is: *'... balanced and broadly based and which:*

promotes the spiritual, moral, cultural, mental and physical development of pupils at the school and of society prepares pupils at the school for the opportunities, responsibilities and experiences of later life.'

Schools in England have a legal responsibility to ensure that teaching is accessible to all, including those who are lesbian, gay, bisexual and transgender (LGBT+). Staff attitudes that promote inclusion and diversity, supported by specific teaching in PSHE, can foster good relations between pupils, tackle prejudice – including transphobia and homophobia – and promote understanding and respect, to enable all members of the school community to flourish.

There is strong evidence that promoting SMSC development throughout the school and supported by good teaching in PSHE can contribute to raising academic standards and improving pupils' life chances. The relationships developed between pupils and their teachers, the ethos of the school, is an essential aspect to improve pupils' learning.

Currently, Ofsted evaluates pupils' SMSC development before making a final judgement on the school's overall effectiveness. Indeed, a school may be judged to have serious weaknesses if the provision for pupils' SMSC development is not at least good.

Despite strong evidence that health education can improve not only children's health but their academic attainment, PSHE is not statutory in maintained schools or academies, and children in primary schools are at the whim of governors as to whether they even have a policy on teaching any aspects around puberty, menstruation or relationships education.

It seems extraordinary that children growing up in a highly sexualised society, for whom pornography is just a few clicks away, and where child sexual exploitation is a constant concern, are not taught simple words for body parts or given an adequate understanding of the physical, social and emotional changes that are likely to happen to them at puberty.

Pressures on schools to deliver on a few, narrow, academic outcomes mean that their statutory duties to promote wellbeing are all too easily overlooked. Despite all the legislation, and Prof. John Hattie's assertion that *"if you want to increase student academic achievement, give each student a friend"*, so many schools still do not spend sufficient time on developing relationships or interpersonal skills. Children's ability to form and maintain relationships contributes to their social and physical wellbeing and their learning but their inter-personal skills also contribute to employability. We know from medicine that the clinician's bedside manner can make a significant impact on prognosis for the patient, but the so-called 'soft skills', which many people seem to find so hard, are seldom taught in schools.

Such skills and attributes are deemed essential by organisations such as the Confederation of British Industry. When employers lament that young people, even post-graduates, are not 'work ready' it should come as no surprise. Although successive governments have flirted with Personal, Social, Health *and Economic* education, employability and enterprise education are no longer part of the national curriculum.

By the end of 2016, five different cross-party parliamentary committees, supported by PSHE experts, teachers and their Unions, the National Association of Head Teachers (NAHT) and parent's groups, had all separately recommended that PSHE, including economic education, should be statutory.

And so to the future …

Some help is, or may be, at hand. On 1st March 2017 the Secretary of State for Education announced plans to make PSHE education statutory in all state-funded schools in England, from September 2019.

Detailed proscription of what schools should teach is unlikely, but evidence-based, theory-driven programmes, must be encouraged to meet the current and future needs of children and young people. Educators, parents, and pupils must engage with public health professionals and politicians to ensure that the interests of children and young people remain central to curriculum reform and improvement. Only then can we have any confidence that children will be better able to keep themselves safe, promote wellbeing and enable them to flourish in every aspect of their lives.

Whole school developmental curricula are needed to help children and young people learn about the essential building blocks for physical health and emotional wellbeing. Effective 'relationships education' is not confined to intimate relationships. A significant majority of young people will go into 'customer-facing' employment, so relationship education must teach them how to collaborate and work successfully in groups; to develop positive long-lasting relationships with people who look, love or worship in ways that are different to them.

Increasingly, relationships will happen online. We must ensure that enabling children and young people to stay safe is not a deficit model but promotes digital citizenship, based on values and skills that promote safe but effective digital communication.

Hard-pressed schools must be supported to fund adequate staff training and enabled to find time in an already busy curriculum to recognise the importance of PSHE, within wider reform of the curriculum and assessment.

Children and young people deserve, and have a right to, values-based education that promotes their SMSC development and their physical and mental wellbeing. They need all adults concerned with the health, wellbeing and achievements to argue actively for curriculum and assessment change. They deserve nothing less.

John Rees taught for 12 years, latterly as a senior leader. John led the transformation of a two-school research project into an effective multi-agency programme with unique evidence of health benefit and educational improvement. An independent educational consultant since 2006, John works with a range of organisations in primary and secondary schools to provide coaching, training and consultancy roles which support school improvement and wellbeing across the UK and overseas. He is passionately committed to enhancing the learning and life chances of children and young people, through school improvement and by supporting the professional development of individuals and organisations.

MAKING IT HAPPEN

Politics, Progress and a Peaceful World

CHAPTER 12

Happy Schools = Successful Students
Is it time for a focus on happy schools?

by Henry Stewart

Imagine a school where staff are energised and motivated by being in control of the work they do. Imagine they feel valued, in the school and beyond, for their professional expertise. Imagine they are trusted and given freedom, within clear guidelines, to decide how to achieve results.

Imagine even that they are not snowed under by workload but have a decent work-life balance. Wouldn't you want to work there? Wouldn't the development and performance of the students be better?

This has not been the direction schools have been going in. Perhaps it is time to shift to a culture of trust in schools, and to a focus on creating an environment where staff feel good about themselves.

In 2015, in a survey of 5,000 teachers, the Guardian Teacher Network found that 98% agreed with the statement: "If staff are happy, students learn better". However, just 37% said they were happy at work. Also, 97% agreed that their teaching is better when they feel trusted. But less than one in three felt trusted at work. Even among headteachers only 39% felt trusted to do the job as they would want to.

"I remember a visitor to Morpeth School coming to me and asking 'why is everybody so happy here?'", commented Sir Alasdair Macdonald, who was headteacher there for many years. "I hadn't really thought about it but I was shocked to realise this was unusual. I think there is a tendency to think that 'Happy Schools' is somehow a soft option, that somehow it's going back to the 80s where we put our arms round children and didn't have high expectations. I don't think it is that at all. We had outstanding Ofsteds, we had very good exam performances, we had very little gaps in terms of pupils. So it is about still having incredibly high expectations."

This is in stark contrast to the statement of Michael Wilshaw, early in his time as Chief Inspector of Ofsted, that "If morale in the staffroom is at an all time low, you must be doing something right".

"I know of no schools where the majority of staff can't be trusted", continues Sir Alasdair "and yet we base our model on the minority, and often it's a tiny minority, who can't."

This situation is not unique to schools. Gallup has famously found that only one in eight employees worldwide feel actively engaged at work. Indeed, in the US, Gallup found that one in six employees are so actively disengaged that "they are miserable in the workplace and destroy what the most engaged employees build".

It doesn't have to be this way. Sir Alisdair describes one key approach: "I think my default position is yes. I think when people come to you with ideas the default position should be yes. I think that immediately creates an environment where people feel supported and encouraged. The default position is often negative.

I've asked thousands of people, in education and beyond, when they have worked at their best. It rarely has anything to do with pay or benefits, or even the level of communication. But it is almost always about being challenged and about being trusted, and given the freedom to decide your own solution. Interestingly most people don't want complete freedom. They like to have clear guidelines to work within, but to be free within those to find their way to do the job.

Here's a simple tip on how to achieve that, which I call "pre-approval". We are all familiar with the idea of being asked to solve a problem, or come up with a new approach, and then bring it back for approval. In this approach, you miss out the last step. When given the task, the individual is pre-approved to implement the idea.

One example of how I've used this was on our website. I'd always been very involved in the website, as it's crucial to the success of my organisation, Happy (which is a training business). I'd "helpfully" get involved, suggesting they get rid of this, add that, and introduce various new features. The result? The person in charge of the website never felt completely in charge of the website, and did not feel trusted or valued.

So with a new website to be created, we decided to pre-approve it. Now let's be clear, that did not mean saying "create whatever you like". It's about freedom within guidelines. We carried out a branding exercise, so the look and feel was clear. We agreed the metrics it would be judged on, namely the number of visitors and how much money it generated. And we made sure Jonny, who was in charge of it, went on the best search engine optimisation training to ensure he had the skills to do the job.

I did not see the proposed site until the evening before it was due to launch, and it was not what I expected. It certainly wasn't what I would have produced. But that is the point. If you truly delegate, you do not get what you would produce. You get what they produce.

However, it was completely within the guidelines and so up it went. A couple of months later we got the data on how it was doing. Visitors had trebled and income had doubled – even without the benefit of my expertise. That is so often the case. If you give somebody real ownership, in an area in which they have the skills, they can often create a far better solution than you could have done.

One primary headteacher in Hillingdon in West London tells me that this approach has changed her life, reduced her stress and given her more time to think strategically. One example she gives is teacher assessment, for which she used to be entirely responsible. After hearing about pre-approval, she delegated the task of teacher assessment, not to the next level down but to the one below. They agreed deadlines and the teachers were pre-approved to find their own solution and implement it – without checking back for approval.

She was a little nervous at first, not knowing what was being discussed and planned. But now they have a new model for assessment, completely owned by those involved and no need for her involvement, which means she has more time to focus on the bigger picture.

I want people at Happy to say "I love going to work. I get to do stuff I'm good at. I am trusted. I know the guidelines but, within them, I am free to work out what to do. I feel valued."

Is that true of your teachers, and your support staff? Do your leadership team and your heads of department see their role not to be the experts, but to help their staff find their own solutions? Do they think each day how they can help their people feel valued?

It is many years since the Department of Education had a policy of "Excellence and Enjoyment". I think it was while David Miliband was Education Minister. But, even within the current climate, there are many schools that do focus on creating great school cultures. There are many schools that believe in order for students to feel happy and achieve well, the teachers need to be happy and feel valued.

One example is Northwold School in Hackney. When Alison Kriel became headteacher, it was underperforming and had teacher attendance below 70%. As part of the turnaround she persuaded governors to approve a staff wellbeing spend, of up to 2% of the school budget. What the budget is spent on ranges from meditation training and massages to staff meals and outings. It may seem hard to find that kind of money with the cutbacks now taking place but, with staff attendance now at 98%, it can be argued to have more than paid for itself.

Of course that budget is only part of the turnaround that has made Northwold one of the best performing primaries in the country. It has all been based on creating a climate of trust. Those managing staff have been trained as coaches, to ensure they are supporting staff to find their own solutions. Being in charge of the school is a role that is rotated, to spread responsibility, with Alison only taking that role one day in six. Staff are given real ownership and feel valued.

Creating a happy school is not about avoiding performance issues. Teachers are generally happier in a school where there is an expectation of professional development and high performance.

Alan Wood led the Learning Trust, which ran education in Hackney as it moved from one of the poorest performing boroughs in 2002 to one of the best performing by the time he retired in 2015.

"Valuing teachers was crucial," he comments. "One of the first things we did was send 20 people a year on an MA teaching course. And we worked hard to ensure teachers learnt from other teachers. In Hackney schools now there is a rich debate about the quality of teaching and the expectation teachers have of each other is much higher."

Is it time for change? Is it time to move away from a focus on school structure and prescription and towards creating great school cultures to enable the best possible learning?

Perhaps these are the sort of questions we should now be asking:

- Can we create a democratic school culture based on learning and reflection, rather than an autocratic one, based on teaching and direction?
- How can we encourage creativity and innovation and step away from a top-down approach?
- How can we create the schools we believe in rather than those we believe Ofsted wants to see?
- How can we build an educational culture based on collaboration, trust and support?

Henry Stewart is CHO (Chief Happiness Officer) of Happy, a learning organisation providing public training, private learning events and bespoke e-learning to organisations. He is also co-founder of the Local Schools Network and was previously Chair of Governors of two Hackney schools.

CHAPTER 13

The Future: Individualised Learning
Machines serving teaching, not teachers as machines

by Jim Knight

We are in an era where even highly-skilled work is under significant threat from the rapid development of intelligent machines. According to the Oxford Study Group, 35 percent of jobs in the UK and 47 percent of the jobs in the US will not exist by 2033. How does a teacher, school leader, or policy-maker know, with confidence, what to prioritise if they are to prepare a child for such an uncertain future? We all must find a new schooling paradigm that prepares every child for a very dynamic workplace, and do it at scale.

Recently, I overheard a five-year-old child in the queue at Costco. She asked her Mum, "What's an algorithm?" Not a question many of us can answer off the cuff, even though they play such a big part in our lives. Google defines it as :"A process or set of rules to be followed in calculations or other problem-solving operations."

Analog algorithms already exist in traditional school classrooms. Teaching to strict lesson plans, to textbooks, to scripts – these are analog teaching algorithms and are now highly replicable in a digital age, largely by machines. They were forged in an industrial era in order to teach content at scale, and were dependent on expensive and highly educated teachers.

The opportunity now is for teachers to deliver a more universal individualised education by being empowered by *digital* algorithms, not enslaved by them.

The current Western model of schooling is neither working well, nor is it scaleable, so it is only natural that we should turn to technology for solutions. Wherever on the spectrum you are – between the algorithmic automation of teaching, and letting children loose with computers as self-directed learners – it seems remarkable that all roads lead to teacherless schooling. There must be a way that retains the profoundly human endeavor of teaching.

The established model of schooling is not only becoming unsustainable in cost and in supply of talented teachers, it will also have to rapidly improve its ability to educate children to higher levels of technical and creative skills. Our schooling systems need to prepare people to effectively compete with machines – or to work effectively alongside them. Can schools use machines to help tackle that challenge?

As an example, Bridge International Academies is delivering low-cost private education in some of the poorest countries of the world, at scale and with positive outcomes in literacy and numeracy test scores. Due to their low-costs, their popularity with parents is reflected in their growth. They are ruthless in driving down costs through economies of scale, and standardised practice. This extends into the classroom where teachers use lesson scripts from tablet computers and managers use data to monitor the progress of each lesson.

For Bridge, the challenge of quickly scaling primary education is being addressed by commissioning experts to design the detailed process of teaching and delivering it through digital algorithms to low-skilled teachers. The reach of a few experts is significantly scaled by a blend of technology and de-skilled teaching. Currently, there's little clarity on how teachers will develop autonomy and thereby professionalism. They are being programmed like machines with algorithms, so why not replace them with machines that will more reliably follow the algorithm?

At the other extreme, Professor Sugata Mitra is trying to tackle the challenge of learning in places where there are few competent teachers. He is investigating the potential of self-organised learning environments and a question-based curriculum. He has shown that children can teach themselves how to use computers and the internet through shared digital resources. As a result, they can effectively acquire knowledge, with adult encouragement and supervision, but without trained teachers. This has not been delivered at anything like the scale of Bridge but it avoids standardisation. It embraces self-directed learning, but does it deliver education? Does it "school" children to behave as their parents and communities would want?

This goes to the broader core question of what we now want from schooling.

Do we want every child to complete schooling and enter adulthood equipped with a canon of knowledge about a broad and balanced curriculum? Should they also have social skills of empathy, communication, and resilience? Do they also need to be creative and skilled in making things as designers, engineers, and performers? What general behaviours do we need children to comply with so that they succeed in living fulfilling lives?

Our whole education system is designed to teach and test individuals in comparison with an "average" ability to recall a standardised curriculum. Those with the best scores go to the best colleges and then get the best jobs. It is a talent-sifting machine created during a time when mass employment was low-skilled and choking human potential was sustainable. But it is inadequate in an era when people are competing against machines and need to maximise their uniqueness.

In *The End of Average*, Todd Rose argues that "today we have the ability to understand individuals and their talents on a level that was not possible before." His attack on the dominant education system is devastating, concluding that "traditional public education systems violate the principles of individuality."

He advocates genuinely individualised learning, which is beyond personalised learning experiences designed to get learners to pass standardised tests. He wants us to move to a tailored learning experience. His answer is to break up qualifications into credentials, to replace grades with competency-based judgments, and to allow learners more self-direction in their learning.

This would create a flexible infrastructure for the sort of system being explored by Sugata Mitra while retaining a place for teachers. Learners would be free to explore their passions. They could obtain credit for what they know, what they make, and what they can do. Their credentials become their individual learning "playlist" that needs no qualification wrapper. This in turn allows potential employers to search beyond the blunt summation of a single grade and find the more precise mix of competencies they need.

This flexible, individualised system may also be scalable. A range of online and face to face learning resources could be used, including more peer learning. There would be better continuity between the experience of social learning in early years and self-directed research in higher education. Employers may also find an improvement in the soft skills they crave such as communication and collaboration – the same human skills that give people a competitive advantage over robots.

What is the role of the teacher in this model? And how can there be confidence that self-directed learners are pushed to be the best they can be in order to realise the potential of their individual talents?

Teachers would remain, chiefly to integrate informal and formal learning. Learners are familiar with digital devices that have no instructions, that are intuitive. They should expect the same from formal learning, and to have the exploration and discovery we enjoy when we uncover the mysteries for ourselves. This shifts the teacher from being an instructor to being more of a collaborator and coach.

Michael Fullan and Maria Langworthy argue in *A Rich Seam* that we need to move teaching from delivery of instructional content to more of a pedagogy of coaching. They identify "a new model learning partnership between and among students and teachers, aiming towards deep learning goals and enabled by pervasive digital access." Whilst this owes much to the likes of Dewey and Montessori, they suggest that these partnerships are now emerging as a result of the interplay between alienated students, disenfranchised educators, and the perpetual advances of digital technology and tools.

The coaching method is fully explored by Daniel Coyle in *The Talent Code*. Instrumental music teachers, sports coaches, and other similar roles train by observing performance, analyzing data, and asking the right questions of each individual so that the work is focused on where improvement is needed.

For example, a great tennis player still needs a coach. Andy Murray is a better tennis player today than Ivan Lendl, but Lendl the coach has played a vital part in Murray's rise to the top through his understanding of the individual. By working on the right parts of Murray's physical and mental game, and by nurturing the growth mindset popularised by Carol Dweck, his tennis performance has been elite.

This pedagogy could be applied to a range of learning and requires human skills not easily converted to algorithms. Facebook is having to hire people to tackle the "fake news" problem, rather than using their world leading algorithm-writing capability. This should give us confidence that interpreting the subtleties and nuances of human communications is hard for machines. Therefore, interpreting the range of visual, cognitive and behavioural signals from a learner is still something we need humans to do.

Every school already employs teachers who are familiar with this approach to teaching sports, the arts, design and technology. They are familiar with subjective forms of assessment that are vested in the expertise of the assessor to judge the competence of performance and exhibition. At schools like the Apollo School in Pennsylvania, they are developing this to create a very different learner experience across the curriculum.

The opportunity is for teachers to evolve these methods at scale. In order to best coach their students and keep their workload manageable, they need the assistance of technology to inform professional judgement.

Rose Luckin and Wayne Holmes argue that artificial intelligence is the new teaching assistant in the classroom. Enhanced data analytics, together with machine learning, offer the promise of significantly enhancing teachers' ability to coach each individual's learning. They also have the potential to capture performance data in real-time, thereby offering a record of ability that can release time and money currently spent on assessment.

AI has implications for teachers wherever they are in the world. Using the digital algorithms behind AI can make previously inconceivable practices possible, transforming our chances of rapidly scaling effective universal education. Ultimately, we have a choice: either we digitise the algorithms of standardisation thus de-professionalizing teachers, or we can develop a new generation of professionals with new approaches, in order to wrap teaching around individual learners.

In modern economies, the current established schooling system is failing too many learners. It is not financially sustainable, teachers are leaving the profession, and child mental health problems are rising. We should not persist with a model that is making our children sick.

A system that believes in, and empowers every child, is possible. It can use latent resources: personal devices, community infrastructure, peer assessment. It can make the teaching profession more sustainable by relieving much of the workload pressure with digital tools and algorithms that can also give teachers insight on their learners, and allow pedagogy to be redefined.

A system that connects learners to their passions can, in turn, connect teachers to the passion of their vocation. Using the algorithm in the service of the teacher, rather than using the teacher to serve the algorithm. We can revive a teaching profession that rediscovers its love – in its practice, in unlocking learning, and in helping all individual children grow.

The original version of this essay was part of the Brookings Series: Meaningful Education in Times of Uncertainty

---

Jim Knight, the Rt Hon Lord Knight of Weymouth, is the Chief Education Adviser at TES Global, having successfully developed their teacher training business. He is also a visiting professor at the UCL Knowledge Lab and a member of the House of Lords. Jim's main policy interests are education, employment, skills and digital technology. He served as an MP from 2001-2009, during which time he was a minister for rural affairs, schools and then employment, with his final year as a Cabinet minister.

Jim is a co-owner of XRapid Ltd, the first company to be commercially selling disease diagnosis using an iPhone app. He is a trustee of the Centre for Accelerating Social Technology and the Jim Cronin Memorial Fund. He is a member of the Government's Digital Engagement Council, the Future of Work Commission established by the Labour Party, and the Brookings Institution's Millions Learning 2.0 Advisory Group.

CHAPTER 14

Working Together is Success
The future lies in cross-sector collaboration

by Neil Roskilly

Growing up as I did in the 1970s under a form of educational apartheid known as the Kent selective system, I never really understood private schools or why anyone would ever attend one. It's not the kind of thing that an unkempt eleven-year-old gives much thought to, being preoccupied, as I was, with surviving the daily commute to my new secondary school's concrete bunker of a bike shed that instilled more fear than the Gates of Mordor, or with avoiding a belligerent PE teacher who would slap you from behind at the slightest excuse (no doubt I gave him lots of excuses!). But the walk home in the evening, if I didn't summon up the courage to cut across the headmaster's garden and save fifteen minutes (caught once, long story, never again), took me past a large house set back from the main road. On the face of it, it seemed indistinguishable from other Edwardian stock, except for a sign outside that announced that it was an independent school. From my limited concrete and glass perspective, it didn't look much like a place of learning.

My mother was a shorthand typist who missed years of school during WW2, and my father was a traditional machine-tool development engineer from the days before university degrees replaced oily rags, so I had no understanding of private schools, what they looked like inside, how many were in captivity or even what you fed them. But the building on the Rochester Maidstone Road seemed a world away from the "toffs and boaters" images of public schools that were regularly splashed across the red-tops at the time, particularly when it suited journalists or politicians to make private education a cause célèbre for some ancient class war.

On the face of it, perhaps little has changed when it comes to the media's portrayal of private education. Except that newspapers of all political persuasions, and not just the working-class titles, now choose to illustrate the latest independent school gossip with images of what to many may seem like bizarre traditions, overly garish uniforms or grandiose buildings. Stock photos regularly include Eton collars and tailcoats, vertical-striped Harrow football shirts that resemble the kit sported by Stanley Matthews, Marlborough College's gothic-style chapel, or Westminster's "Greaze", where some poor pancake is mauled to shreds in the presence of the Dean. It's no wonder that the majority, for whom self-funded education is a mystery, end up with a somewhat jaundiced view of the private sector as one of separation and indulgence. Dollop in the mandatory quote of annual fees well north of the price of a new Fiat ("£180,000 – 13 years of London private school fees", Financial Times, 2/9/16) and it's no wonder that there's often a sharp intake of breath if privately-funded schooling is mentioned. Even the many who have enjoyed positive experiences of independent education can still be a little defensive whenever it gets a mention.

Outside of a rare crisis, of the 1,863 independent schools registered in England, only a handful have ever featured in the national media. So, ask the public to name three private schools and they may very well suggest Eton, Harrow and Hogwarts. While fees at the school of witchcraft and wizardry remain undisclosed, for every high-fee "public" school that regularly gets a mention in the press, there are hundreds of relatively inexpensive neighbourhood private schools that remain largely hidden from view. These contribute significantly to the employment base and local educational matrix, and often fill gaps in state provision in areas such as the performing arts and special needs.

Perhaps surprisingly, the fees charged by these schools can be similar to the per-pupil funding received by maintained schools, and often less than the annual nursery childcare fees that many parents with young families now face. Even in wealthy Caterham, Surrey, Oakhyrst Grange School charges around £6,000 annually and St. Nicholas House School in North Walsham charges about £5,000, asking parents for around one-third of the oft-quoted "average" of £16,296.[16] Such fees will still be prohibitive for many, but the headlines that our private schools are becoming the sole preserve of foreign oligarchs are unrepresentative.

Of course, some private schools charge eye-watering fees and will always be the domain of the wealthy, despite increasing numbers of bursaries supporting children from disadvantaged backgrounds. However, the "House" or "Grange" in the name of many of Britain's independent

---

[16] "ISC Census and Annual Report 2017". The Independent Schools Council.

schools often points to their relatively humble origins, where small-scale and relatively low-cost enterprises operated by charitable trusts or proprietors still flourish. These are the modern-day successors to the Board Schools described by Conan Doyle as "Lighthouses, my boy! Beacons of the future! Capsules with hundreds of bright little seeds in each, out of which will spring the wiser, better England of the future."

If the public's imperfect perception of Britain's private school sector is understandable, perhaps our legislators should at least be aware of the variety of species out there in the wild. After all, rarely does a parliamentary week go by without some educational call to arms, either seeing private schools as the answer to all our prayers or as the spawn of the devil. There will always be political detractors of course, particularly if a few well-endowed schools resist doing more to justify their charitable tax-breaks and public benefit, but many of our politicians operate an outmoded view of the sector that seems to shed more shadow than light.

Just under half of all parents aspire to private education, believing that the high-stakes accountability model that dominates state education in England can stifle innovation, narrow the curriculum, and focus increasingly strained resources at the organisational level rather than the individual child. Parents also recognise that through wider and extra-curricular programmes, independent schools encourage the development of mental toughness and resilience, particularly in areas such as commitment and challenge, further encouraging openness to experience and remaining positive in the face of challenge. These soft skills are also the most important factors employers weigh up when recruiting school and college leavers, with attitude to work (valued by 89%) followed by aptitude for work (66%) ranking well ahead of formal qualifications (23%).[17]

Even where politicians see our private schools as part of the solution rather than the problem, policy formulation tends to focus on the impractical. The 2016 Education Green Paper suggested that around 100 private schools could directly sponsor academies or Free Schools. Previous adventures in this area have produced a mixed bag, with some notable successes and failures, but without any real evidence of improved pupil outcomes overall.

While inspection outcomes rarely tell the full story, Theale Green School, an academy in Reading sponsored by independent Bradfield College, was judged as "Requires Improvement" at its May 2017 inspection, as was Oxford's Windale Community Primary School in January 2017, sponsored by The Dragon. There's no fault on either side here as the two sectors' needs are just different, despite the common element of children. This is where legislators and their advisors often come a cropper. It's a bit like asking Ginger Rogers to direct the orchestra while dancing with Fred Astaire, famously backwards and in high heels, while the conductor remains stage right, baton still in top pocket.

Perhaps unsurprisingly, Dulwich College, an independent school in south London, pulled out of sponsoring an academy in 2013, claiming its staff were not equipped to help pupils at a state school. The notion that private schools can improve academies *is* built on the laudable view of a common moral purpose, but it has yet to

---

[17] "The Right Combination: CBI/Pearson Education and Skills Survey 2016". Confederation of British Industry: July 2016.

deliver on systemic and sustained scalable improvements. Despite both being engaged in educating the children of Britain, the state and private sectors, through years of unfortunate separation, have evolved into distinct species and it's a misconception that they can now mate easily, if you forgive the pun.

Yet this isn't to argue that there's little or no overlap in the venn diagram. While as of March 2017 only eleven organisations had been set up by independent schools for the purpose of sponsoring academies and free schools, hundreds more were engaged in small-scale inter-school partnerships with the potential to make a real difference to the life chances of many children in this country. Like most private schools in the UK, these are enterprises that rarely fall under the national media's spotlight. This isn't just the sharing of facilities, but curriculum or wider community-based initiatives with a common desire to bring the sectors together, harnessing expertise on both sides in a mutually-beneficial relationship. It's the equal footing of partners that promises to keep Fred and Ginger upright, not a one-sided dependency where the initial flame is all too commonly extinguished by expediency and changing obligations. Like Jean Giorno's shepherd planting acorns in Provence, these modest undertakings promise to create a verdant forest, one tree at a time.

And partnerships between state and independent schools are certainly flourishing. There are over 1,750 projects recorded nationwide, covering everything from digital inclusion to sports, STEM education, holiday clubs and governance.[18] It's an exchange of expertise

---

[18] https://www.schoolstogether.org

that promises to revolutionise how schools work on the ground. These aren't just casual bilateral arrangements, but sustainable multi-partner schemes harnessing expertise from all involved. For example, under the government's Cadet Expansion Programme (CEP), Medway (Kent) now has Gad's Hill (independent), Brompton Academy and Medway University Technical College (state) in partnership.

Not far away in South-west London, eight schools (seven in the state sector) operate a thriving drama consortium that recently brought "The Pilgrim of Love" to the stage. Involving 150 pupils, the show's message of reconciliation across faiths promises to create lasting respect across the community. Back in the classroom, the Canterbury Primary Science Partnership (CPSP) involves eleven state and private schools engaging through teacher-training as well as workshops and "shows" for KS1 and KS2 pupils on topics such as the planets and gravity. At the same time, Year 7 children from across York come together regularly in focus groups debating topics such as the greatest breakthrough in human history, including the relative merits of fire, numbers, the Enigma Code, the aqueduct, the printing press and, very appropriately, the planting of the first seed.

Harnessing outside expertise and other organisations can also act as an important catalyst in meaningful private-state partnerships. Loughborough Lightning's international netball stars are running joint training sessions for private and state schools in the catchment around Long Eaton, as well as further afield into Nottinghamshire and Derbyshire, while the English Football Association brings the Women's FA Cup for an appearance alongside 300 girls from state and independent schools at the annual ISA Football Festival.

Independent Dixie Grammar, and Ellesmere College – a special school on the outskirts of Leicester City – are using the Duke of Edinburgh's Scheme to help more children qualify at Bronze level. The two schools are also collaborating on environmental projects in support of Aylestone Meadows, a 271-acre Local Nature Reserve that forms a green wedge within the city boundary. Over on the Isle of Wight, a hub of primary and secondary schools, including Greenmount, St Blasius, Dover Park and Binstead (all state) collaborate with Ryde Junior School (private) in hosting the annual IOW Literary Festival for both pupils and teachers. Throughout the country, state and private schools are enjoying collaborations that are not only breaking down barriers but also helping to create solutions to local need. Conan Doyle's beacons of the future, indeed.

Even if examples of partnerships are legion, do they make a long-term difference? While only representing a fraction of the total number of collaborations, the Department for Education's (DfE) July 2017 report on eighteen primary curriculum projects, involving over 230 staff from across 112 schools and approximately 4,220 pupils, commented on the "positive changes in achievement, attitude and confidence for the subjects pupils were learning".[19] Given the current pressure on resources, these "partnerships were a cost-effective means of developing relationships between the two school sectors". While long-term evaluations of the

---

[19] Bourne, Mike. "Independent State School Partnerships (ISSP) – impact of and lessons learnt. Research report." Department for Education: July 2017.

impact on pupil attainment have yet to be established, DfE concludes that "the signs are promising".

Of course, it is often the immeasurable differences that really matter in education, not just standard and often-disputed headline gauges of children's progress and attainment. If these burgeoning partnerships between maintained and independent schools can help to challenge the artificial barriers often lazily perpetrated by the media, encourage greater engagement and further increase understanding via collaboration, then our children will be in a better position to thrive in a post-Brexit UK. In a country often characterised by its segregated approach to education, the maturing of cross-sector partnerships offers true hope for the future. This has finally been recognised by legislators who have acknowledged that the lack of a central brokerage service has meant that partnerships have not always been established where they can make the most impact. The Department for Education's new System Partnership unit aims to help educators identify where existing expertise can be shared, as well as evaluating the impact of schemes across the country. Its success isn't guaranteed of course, as any sense of a disproportionate relationship between the sectors will enforce rather than dispel the preconceptions that have become entrenched over many years of partisan media depiction.

Cross-sector partnerships aren't a magic bullet to the country's educational challenges, of course. But they do offer ground-floor opportunities of collaboration that can address local inequalities and grow understanding, as much among our legislators as potentially with parents and pupils; even for the average eleven-year-old walking the Rochester Maidstone Road. And any future for the UK's education system has to be stronger with educators working in partnership. As Henry Ford said, "coming together is a beginning; keeping together is progress; working together is success".

Neil Roskilly is Chief Executive of ISA, the membership association that represents 430 independent schools. The association has seen membership growth of 70% over the last seven years and is now one of the most influential organisations in the sector. Neil advises DfE, HMRC and a range of examination bodies on educational policy. Neil served on the General Teaching Council for England, is a Board Member for the Independent Schools Council, and trustee of 'We', and the charity 'Beat', helping children affected by eating disorders. Neil taught in maintained and private sectors, is an experienced headteacher and governor, and regularly comments on educational matters in the media.

CHAPTER 15

School Leadership without Fear

by David Jackson

"Leaders have to be engaged at the heart level in order to be courageous champions."

Margaret Wheatley

There are many definitions of leadership and maxims about it, so for this piece I'm going to appropriate one or two. Why? Because what we perceive leadership to be inevitably conditions how we believe it should be enacted.

What does it mean to lead?

For those of us who lead in the professional context of education, I see it as being a pretty high calling. It is not a position or a status. It is a role bestowed upon us by those who entrust their custodianship (trustees or governors) and followership (staff and parents) upon us. Ultimately, therefore, it is something earned by the quality and integrity of our enacted leadership. It's not a role thing or a position thing. It's a lived thing.

What that means in practice is that a group of professionals, whose values have called them to work in school (because they are passionate to be in the changing lives business), entrust their experience to the leadership of the headteacher. The fulfilment of their mission is largely dependent upon the degree to which it is enabled by the leader of their school.

So far so good!

My belief is that we have lost the boldness of this calling. That leadership in schools is too much about managing public accountability; that we have sidelined our values; that too many leaders have such fear for their jobs that they compromise on what they truly believe; that we are selling short those professionals who passionately care – and in so doing diminishing ourselves and the educational mission. That we need more courageous leadership.

Integrity, vision and hope

So, let's take a few loosely attributed quotes about leadership:

> *"Management is doing things right; leadership is doing the right things"*

> *"The supreme quality for leadership is unquestionably integrity"*

> *"A leader is one who knows the way, goes the way, and shows the way"*

> *"Leadership is the capacity to translate vision into reality"*

> *"Leadership is not about a title or a designation. It's about impact, influence and inspiration"*

> *"A leader is a dealer in hope. Where there is no vision, there is no hope"*

These are variously from Warren Bennis, Dwight Eisenhower, John Maxwell, Robin Sharma, Peter Drucker and Napoleon Bonaparte. Great leadership has both a moral compass – it stands for something that really matters – and it has vision. The two are linked because people get inspired by the moral foundation of leadership as it forms itself into narratives and images that cohere into a vision of what is possible. Good leaders are storytellers and vision shapers.

It is not the task here to portray the vision for schools. That's what leaders do. A vision is categorically, though, not "outstanding in our next Ofsted", or "improving our Key Stage 2 or Key Stage 4 results", or "getting the borderline candidates over the bar", or "managing our admissions so that we protect our results".

It is much more likely to be housed in an ambition for the role of the school in enriching and deepening the experience for the local community; or in transforming the life chances for all learners (but in particular the most vulnerable and underserved); or in liberating the agency of all in the school – adults and young people – around serving one another and the world. These are higher order ambitions than Ofsted grades, and they are examples of the stuff of leadership. Too many of our school leaders seem to have lost their way, their nerve or their perspective of the leader they really want to be.

Inspiring and leading through others

Time for a few quotes again…

> "Leadership is unlocking people's potential to become better"

> "The function of leadership is to produce more leaders, not more followers"

> "Leadership is infinite. Great leaders draw from a seemingly bottomless well"

And, differently...

*"We have been assigned this mountain to show others
that it can be moved"*

These are variously from Stephen Covey, Bill Bradley,
Ralph Nader and 'anonymous'. The bottom line is that
what they all say, in one form or another, is that great
leaders in pursuit of bold goals create shared enterprise,
liberate potential, ignite the flame of passion in others and
build leadership capacity – the irresistible capacity to move
mountains together.

Some years ago a school leader friend, Chris Cotton,
and I wrote a published piece together that we called "The
Spaces Between the Pebbles in a Jar". Basically, he provided
the metaphor and I wrote the piece, but his was the more
profound contribution. Chris' thesis was that leadership is
not enshrined in structure, position or power relationships.
Instead, it is a variable and fluid capacity, and it flows
within and beyond an organization – it fills the spaces
between the pebbles.

For the leader, this is a creative challenge. One of the
myths of what we have come to call 'distributed leadership'
is that it equates with delegation and is bestowed 'down'
an organisation. It doesn't. Delegation is a manifestation
of power relationships. Expanding the flow of leadership is
about *empowerment* – opportunity, space, support, capacity
and growth. Jobs and tasks are 'delegated' (passed down
a managerial structure) but leadership is liberated and
allowed to find its own space.

Such fluid opportunities not only liberate leadership,
they are emancipatory for the person in the professional.
Those who work in schools give of who they are as well

as what they do. The release and expression of potential through leadership creates the context for both personal and professional fulfilment. Leading the growth of leadership capacity is thus intensely human and social, an emotionally intelligent activity.

Leadership as described above is an infinite, not a finite thing. Leaders can grow it within their organisations and they do so by inviting people into the spaces so they can achieve great things. As Linda Lambert says, 'everyone has both the potential and the entitlement to contribute towards leadership'. In so doing we ennoble the educational enterprise and fulfil those we work with. And boy does our profession need some of that currently!

But there is another essential piece to this section. How on earth, in the current context, do you create schools that feel and function like this? It may sound good, but heads have to live in the real world. True. We live in the real world that we create. We can be victims of the wider context or we can be the creative designers of our own reality.

Some years ago, in the 1990s, Joseph Murphy acted as an evaluator in the United States for some of the country's most ambitious schools – those within the New American Schools Programme. As one outcome of that, he wrote a book on the modern principalship in which he constructed a set of alternative contemporary metaphors for school leadership. They have been adapted a little for this piece, but the essence of Murphy's metaphors survive:

New Metaphors for School Leadership

School leader as shaper of culture

    …. as moral agent
    …. as organisational architect

.... as social architect

.... as educator

.... as advocate for children

.... as community builder

.... as servant

.... as leadership capacity creator

All of which – holding onto a bold vision and liberating the capacity to achieve it – take us to the final section: turning all this into action.

TURNING VISION INTO ACTION

Re-imaginer and re-designer – the moral purpose

There is a legitimate image of the education system as being a form of UK Education plc. Effectively then, a corporately-run enterprise with 24,000 local branches, much like a major bank, or supermarket chain, or Starbucks, each school compliant to the corporate design, values and operational procedures. In such a world, national policy dictats, Ofsted inspections and public accountability expectations are the means to keep the system compliant and relatively standardised. In such a world, school leaders are primarily the intermediate managers ensuring the ship runs efficiently and effectively within these corporate parameters. Managers first, leaders second.

Yet there is another view. This one says that there is no desire to standardise the system. In fact, it says, the whole thrust of policy has been to liberate schools to create their own unique ethos and design, consistent with the local context and the ambitions of the school leader and the community (school and local). It says that UK headteachers have been given unprecedented freedoms and autonomy and that the only checks and balances (other than fiscal probity) sit with public accountability expectations applied to all schools, and the Ofsted framework – and that these are as constraining or as liberating as each leader chooses to fashion them.

It will be obvious which of these world views I favour. But this second scenario doesn't go far enough. There are two further dimensions of this leadership freedom beyond having the creative opportunity to lead as we might wish. The first involves reimagining the school; the second reimagining the system.

Reimagining 'school'

'School leader as moral agent and organisational architect' obviously means shaper of the design, creator of enabling conditions, entrepreneur of time and space. But there is a broader and bolder sense in which this is true.

Our model of schooling is more than 100 years old and it is way out of date. The rest of society – our industrial practices, technology, the media we use, our leisure activities, communication systems – has undergone a revolution. There has been a similar revolution in our approaches to adult education. For example, since the 1960s, the Open University has demonstrated that virtually every adult is capable of degree-level study, given the right learning approaches and modes of assessment. More than three million people, most failed by their schooling, have now passed OU degrees. By contrast, our schools have hardly changed at all.

And yet this highly durable school model has singularly failed to achieve equitable outcomes, or to address socio-economic disadvantage, or to fully engage most learners. More profoundly, it has failed to equip all learners with a graduation entitlement of positive self-esteem, an affirming portfolio and a desire to continue learning throughout life. It has also notably failed to provide teachers with an intellectually and emotionally challenging and fulfilling professional context, or actively involved parents in the learning experiences of their children. And all this should not be a big ask – it should be the purpose of school, a moral entitlement for all.

The original purpose of school – designed to sort and sift, to separate sheep and goats – is now redundant. We need 100% of students to be skilled and capable citizens, able to contribute positive agency to both their economic and social world.

Our UK government (and other governments around the world) is still flogging the dead horse of the out-of-date school model when it is patently incapable of responding to the challenges set out above. And it isn't the fault of the students (many of whom go on in adulthood to achieve success well beyond their schools' predictions). It is the fault of the model of schooling, and no amount of Ofsted inspection, or examination rigour and reform, or teacher performance management, can make an out-of-date model fit for our times.

So what exactly is so wrong with this particular dead horse? Well, we have lived with the badly-functioning model of schooling for so long that we rarely ask ourselves obvious, glaring questions, like:

- Why have we retained so exclusively the subject-based curriculum, when no tasks in the real world segregate knowledge or its applications in that way?

- Why do we assess all students at the same time, rather than when they are ready to demonstrate mastery (think music grades, or driving test, or sports coaching awards, or Open University modules, or PhD dissertations)?

- Why do we still have rigid age-cohorting? It certainly isn't because we believe that all students mature and progress at the same rates. Watch rehearsals for a school production or a concert if you wonder about mixed-age learning.

- Why are schools designed into corridors and classroom spaces such that it makes teaching the most isolated and un-stimulating of professional practices?

- Why do most schools set 'homework', when they already have students in school for 35 hours a week – and when the world outside school is rich in opportunities for self-initiated learning?

- Why do most schools have 25 one-hour lessons when nobody can believe that it is a unit that is enabling of deep or applied learning?

- Why is the assessment outcome that matters still an exam written by pen on paper and marked by anonymous paid markers when teachers know students and their capabilities from five years of engagement with them?

- Does speaking matter? Do so-called hard skills matter? Do so-called soft skills matter? Does making and doing matter? If so, why are none of these things given higher currency?

- Why do we persist with the corrosive language and practice of 'ability' groupings? Schools are the only places where it is deemed appropriate to classify people as 'low ability' or 'less able'.
- And given that schools are centres of learning, why are the adult learning norms and practices in many of our schools so poor?

Some of the most innovative, future-focused schools in the US – including High Tech High, Big Picture Learning and New Tech Network – asked themselves these questions and created alternative school models that share the following characteristics:

- All include interdisciplinary and applied learning (project-based learning; 'maker' assignments; real world tasks; internships) – some engaging and empowering pedagogical models which, not incidentally, require teachers to collaborate as designers and facilitators.
- All focus on the centrality of relationships. They have 'advisory', where advisory is viewed as 'the soul of the school', embodying support for students as higher order than teaching the curriculum.
- All have powerful and sustained and participative adult learning norms that model the learning practices undertaken with students.
- All have pervasive cultural identity and school-level ownership of what matters, including what is assessed, and how and by whom it is assessed.

Reimagining the 'system' – educational above institutional leadership

A few years ago, I presented at a headteachers' workshop in a challenging northern city. They were frustrated about perceived imperfections in the Local Authority and the subsequently contracted out private sector delivery organisation. I presented an outline of how a system might function collaboratively and collegially: how they could unite around some shared principles and agree policy and strategy together, how it was possible to deploy expertise across schools and personnel to places of most need, and how they could learn from, with and on behalf of one another. We walked through the dynamics of a collegiate and collaborative system aligned around collective responsibility for all children.

When I asked whether they wanted their system to be more like that, they were confounded. They would, of course, but they couldn't imagine how it could be made to happen – from where the leadership would come. I pointed out that the educational leadership in that city was gathered in the room. From where else was the leadership to come? It just needed to be translated from institutional concerns to higher order collegial educational concerns – a shared commitment to the success of every child in the city. In fact it just needed some leaders to step up with a bold and compelling vision of what was possible, and an invitational offer for others to engage in active and participatory and collectively courageous followership. And some of them did just that.

Our UK system is in flux. There has never been such a rich opportunity for school leaders to take hold of the agenda and reimagine what is possible across a local system of schools. It starts, of course, with those of us privileged to lead getting in touch again with our true passions as our first priority – to be "engaged at the heart level" as Margaret Wheatley says – so that we can lead without fear.

David Jackson has expertise in education, leadership, organization and system change. David was headteacher of Sharnbrook Upper School and Community College for 14 years. Subsequently, he was appointed a founding director at the National College for School Leadership. He has taught on Leadership Masters programmes at Cambridge and Nottingham universities and worked on school and system change initiatives in a number of countries. Since 2010 David has been a Senior Associate at the UK's Innovation Unit where he has supported: Learning Futures, Global Education Leaders, New York City's iZone and Australia's Learning Frontiers initiatives. Most recently David has been working to establish ExL Trust – a Multi Academy Trust of new school models.

CHAPTER 16

Pedagogies of Peace and Power

by Debra Kidd

In this book, Guy Claxton asks us to consider, among many other important considerations, the outcomes an education system generates in order to create a more peaceful world. It is impossible to engage with the possibility of such a peaceful future without considering the role of empathy and compassion in education, or indeed, to create the thriving, innovative future that other writers in this book have advocated, without considering the need for wisdom.

In *Against Empathy*[20] – a book with far more nuance than its title suggests – Paul Bloom argues that our belief that empathy makes for a better world is flawed. It is not empathy, he argues, but rational compassion that makes the difference. It is perfectly possible to understand another's feelings and yet fail to do anything to improve their situation. We might take issue with the idea that compassion can be rational in the light of what we know about how feelings impact on decision-making from Antonio Damasio[21] and others, but the fact remains that feeling alone will not

[20] Bloom, P (2017) *Against Empathy: The case for Rational Compassion*, Bodley Head, Penguin, London.
[21] Damasio, A (2005) *Descartes Error* (2nd Ed paperback), Penguin, London.

improve the lot of others. In another book, *The Empathy Instinct,*[22] Peter Bazalgette acknowledges this important distinction between empathy and compassion, but makes the case that one is built upon the other, and so it is not a matter of being against empathy, but rather a matter of setting a direction and understanding how the critical ingredient of empathy can be put to altruistic ends.

These wranglings about the definitions of empathy are problematic enough without education systems across the world assuming that empathy is not the domain of the teacher or school – that it is either something you have or don't have, or that it can't or even shouldn't be taught. You'll not find politicians arguing that they don't want children to care. But they often seem to conflate care with obedience and compliance.

As education systems across the world argue about whether skills or knowledge should take precedence; as social media bubbles debate progressive versus traditional pedagogies – as binary positions become more entrenched into 'rights' and 'wrongs' and as governments obsess about international comparisons – children and teachers continue to work together in classrooms, distracted from bigger goals by the immediacy of tests. If religion was once deemed to be the opium of the masses, high-stakes test results have become the crack cocaine of the education system. Best intentions have become reduced to performative outcomes linked to ever narrowing criteria. Ideologies, arguments, competition, global issues, the needs of humanity and of our planet become reduced to tests that allow us to don

---

[22] Bazalgette, P (2017) *The Empathy Instinct*, John Murray, London

the comforting cloak of certainty without actually effecting change.

Yet deep down, we all know that once the basics of literacy and numeracy are secured, it is the immeasurables that make the biggest difference to children's lives. Their capacity to connect, to build positive relationships, to listen, to reason, to act wisely and with compassion are traits that lead not only to more successful lives but to more joyful ones too. We can smile and nod at the Harvard study conclusion that 'happiness is love', and agree with Aristotle and Seligman[23] that happiness is inextricably linked with a sense of value and purpose that is rooted in community and relationships, but where is the pedagogy for such a life? How can it be purposefully built into the fabric of education?

Research into empathy at the Max Planck Institute by Tania Singer[24] shows that our ability to empathise is deeply connected to our own sense of wellbeing. Self regulation, positive emotions, taking time to make decisions in a considered way – all these improve our abilities to override our tribal instincts and to empathise with others. We can practice and improve our capacity to empathise, but our own state of mind is critical. To this end, the researchers at the Institute have found that practices such as mindfulness

---

[23] Seligman, M (2009 – reprint) *Authentic Happiness – Using the New Positive Psychology to Realise Your Potential for Deep Fulfilment*, Nicholas Brierley, Boston.

[24] Singer, T., & Tusche, A. (2013). Understanding others: Brain mechanisms of Theory of Mind and empathy. In P. W. Glimcher (Ed.), *Neuroeconomics. Decision making and the brain*. London, UK: Academic Press.

and meditation improve empathy and our willingness to act with compassion.

We read in this book and elsewhere of the challenges facing our children in the future and the need for them to be adaptive, innovative and wise. Compassion is a key element of this, as is the capacity to view a problem from multiple perspectives. But what we don't want children to feel is that the future is full of danger, and that they will be pitched against others in a battle for survival. There's a real danger, at this present time, that this is what is happening. Whether it is in the stories of other countries doing better in tests, to growing anti-immigration narratives, our children are at a cross-roads. Exclude or include. Compete or collaborate. Reject or rejoice. Mope or Hope. Pedagogies of peace take children through a process in which the latter option is the best. Pitching together not against.

We know from cognitive science and beyond that stories are particularly privileged in the human mind. Willingham,[25] drawing on E.M Forster, speaks of the powerful combination of character, conflict, causality and complications in imbuing stories with powerful memories. Taking these stories to place children in the shoes of others, to our minds, creates a learning experience like no other, particularly when those stories take them on a journey where they wade knee deep through dilemma. Where what they thought was true is questioned; where sometimes the people they sided with turned out to be flawed, and vice versa. Where, in the words of the International

---

[25] Willingham, D (2004) The Priviledged Status of Story, Americal Federation of Teachers, available from http://www.aft.org/periodical/american-educator/summer-2004/ask-cognitive-scientist

Baccalaureate, they learn "that other people, with their differences, can also be right." For if they can learn this, yes, they can pass tests but they can also impact on the world in more positive and humane ways.

What if as we celebrate the death of Medusa, praising our hero, Perseus, we take time to consider why she was hiding in a cave in the first place? How had she become a monster? Who is the hero and what is a monster?

What if, as we write an 'optimistically truthful' report on a dilapidated mansion house, hidden deep in a forest for our anonymous client, we find out that his name is Count Dracula?

What if, as another one of our heroes, carrying home the head of our foe – the Jabberwock – we receive a message from a neighbouring tribe that the creature was sacred to their way of life and our actions a sacrilege – even an act of war?

What if … the two most powerful words in the world.

When we're teaching children about the acceptance of 'otherness' it's not enough to see the unfamiliar and to pull that unfamiliar into the known – to make the other 'one of us' in order to feel compassion. Doing this tends to create a set of conditions: you are one of us as long as you conform to our rules and norms. We'll accept you as long as you are deserving. Such models of empathy lead to notions such as 'the deserving poor' and they allow us to exclude while looking like we're inclusive. Just look at the explosion of zero tolerance schools where behaviour policies are so draconian that only the most compliant survive. Or academy chains with expensive uniforms and strict policies of enforcement that drive poorer families away. Or those with parental contracts so detailed that only the most committed and capable families dare apply. These rules of compliance ride in on a horse of compassion and they are anything but. So in the classroom, children need to learn how power works, how coercion works, how propaganda works, how guilt and shame are utilised to control. And they need to do this with joyfulness and excitement. Hmmm. Let's take a quick look at the start of our unit on Perseus...

We're sitting in class, tables back and chairs facing the front. I am in role as King Acrisius of Argos and I am cross. My class have been told that they are his advisers; that he has been absent for months consulting the oracle, and that on his return he has dragged them out of their beds to share a problem. They have been warned that he is a difficult man and they should take care when speaking to him.

From the outset the children are set in a challenging power dynamic.

The king tells his advisers that the oracle has informed him that the son of his daughter, Danae, will grow to kill him. He is outraged and demands that his advisers come up with a solution to ensure this does not happen. And thus we enter the story of Perseus.

The immediacy of the problem distracts the children from the ethics of the request. Power and convention are playing their roles in forcing compliance and obedience.

We need to step out of the story for a moment or two to gather some facts. What was the oracle? Where was Argos? What was a city state? Where are we in time? What do the children already know about Ancient Greece? They share their knowledge and we gather it into categories:

knowledge about beliefs, myths, ways of life, geography and power. Then we return to our story.

Pedagogically speaking, knowledge is important here, but only insofar as it drives the desire and need to understand. The task forms the purpose in which the knowledge is acquired, but it is also universal AND particular – particular to the historical context, universal to the human condition, exploring themes of power, agency and control.

The advisers are given some time to present to Acrisius their solutions. The children must present their ideas in a way that is respectful to the king. They must think carefully about language and gesture. They must also remember that the king loves his daughter and that she is only about 12 years old. These constraints ensure that the children don't immediately suggest killing the child. They also ensure that they heighten their language and use a formal register.

The King (the teacher) is forcing control. Pleasing the oppressor becomes more important than protecting the child. The extent to which we blindly follow orders is something we can discuss as a class later on.

And so on.

The story allows us to confront uncomfortable issues from a distance. The children are enjoying the story and are engaged, but they are exploring the nature of power. We can come back to these issues with philosophical inquiry, drama, writing…but the process is playful. They are safe, protected but provoked and challenged. Finding this balance is not easy. But then neither is changing the world.

Behind most of our stories are deep philosophical questions. There are those in plain sight. There are those hidden ones, shrouded by assumption and habit – the ones that need to be gently exposed. Teacher and child working like archeologists to painstakingly brush the dust off the assumption. These kinds of questions take empathy well beyond feeling. They take it into the realm of wisdom and into what Hywel Roberts calls 'botherdness' – where education really begins to matter. And when education matters, it becomes material. It changes the state of things. It carries with it the potential for a more positive and peaceful future, even if the peace is not quiet.

Debra Kidd has worked in education for 25 years. An Associate for the RSA and for Independent Thinking Ltd, she is the author of two books: *Teaching: Notes from the Frontline* and *Becoming Mobius.* A third with Hywel Roberts, *Uncharted Territories: Great Adventures in Learning* is due out at the end of the year. She is a columnist for Teach Primary and a regular writer for Teach Secondary and co-founder and organiser of Northern Rocks – one of the largest teaching and learning conferences in the UK. She has a doctorate in education, blogs regularly and believes more than anything else that the secret to great teaching is "Make it Matter".

CONCLUSION

What's Next?

We believe that the time is right for a social movement, one that challenges the narrow conversation we've been having for decades about standards and structures. Instead of arguing whether tests are too hard or too soft, or whether schools should be run by trusts, local authorities or parents, we think we should be discussing how schools should help our kids prepare for a turbulent and fast-changing world. We began this book by identifying ten issues around which to build that conversation, but there are probably many more that you can think of.

We've tried to identify what a future-focused programme of change would need to address. If you've been inspired by the ideas put forward, we hope you will become involved by helping to forge this movement.

How you can stay involved and help build a movement for change

The prime purpose of this book is to start making waves around the idea of transforming our schools so they're fit for the future, to set out why this is needed, and to outline ways in which the educational experiences and outcomes for young people could be better. For that reason we've deliberately addressed multiple audiences – parents, young people and community members as well as politicians, educational leaders and teachers.

The point, though, is that the book is not the thing. Its ambition is the thing. If it is a success, it will be because of the energy it generates and the permission that it gives to diverse voices to step up and to be heard. As a group we need to become more diverse, in every sense, but we thought that the most important thing was to start. We could have spent a couple of years establishing committees, seeking approval from existing advocacy groups, sounding-out political party support, and making sure our contributors reflected all sectors of education and wider society. But almost all of us have been involved in campaigns like that and they almost always collapsed before they began, through fatigue and fear of criticism. We don't fear criticism, what we aim to do is ask critics to join us in a productive conversation rather than a divisive one. Our starting point is to get some ideas out there, and see if there's sufficient support for those ideas that others will want to take forward. No-one has been paid (quite the reverse!) and we have no professional staff or organisation. So, the task, for the group of writers and associates uniting round the theme of Education Forward is now to invite others to join in.

With that in mind we have established the following (initial) platforms:

A website: www.educationforward.co.uk. Here, you'll find all of these essays, published under a Creative Commons 'Share and Attribute' License.

Twitter: Use #educationforward to express your support (or disagreement!)

Facebook: www.facebook.com/Education4ward

What you can do to be the change you want to see

If you do *nothing* else, pass this book to someone else and ask them to read it. The majority of the issues discussed in this book don't need permission from anyone in order to implement them. A few can be addressed only by policy-makers, but this won't happen unless enough of us insist upon them happening.

Students:

- You are the ones whose lives are being determined by the existing system of schooling. If you don't like it, make your opinion count. Don't worry that expressing your view will damage your prospects at school; the chances are that your teachers and school leaders feel exactly the same way you do. They will welcome your support. And, it's all part of your education to question the systems around you. Ask 'Why do we do it this way?' and 'Could we do this better? If so, how?'.

- Remember that the people who currently look after your interests have had very little influence, politically, in the shape of educational policy. Don't blame them for the way things are – instead, recognise that we are where we are, and that we have to work within those constraints. If you like going to school, make sure you let your teachers know it. If you don't, work with them, and with your parents, to change it.

- Despite all the pressure heaped upon you by the media when exams come around, bear in mind that employers these days largely hire on attitude, not test scores. Do your best at exam time, but remember that – like passing your driving test – you may never take another exam once you're done with formal education. The first 20% of your life bears little or no resemblance to the remaining 80%. We wish it were otherwise but until that day comes, keep it in perspective. Many of the contributors in this book hated school, but they managed to do just fine in life.

- Encourage your teachers to teach you things that AREN'T in the exam syllabus. Give them moral support to go off-piste and to innovate.

School leaders:

- Work with fellow headteachers locally to make your area's schools 'future-literate'. Forward-looking issues differ from those that are top of the current agenda. Such things as budgets, changes to exam specifications and staff shortages can be difficult to manage, but recognise that they are immediate rather than longer term.

- Headteachers in many communities meet their MPs regularly, and most MPs take this forum seriously and use this opportunity to discuss the big picture. However, politicians have become adept at coping with complaints about the national situation either by supporting or explaining and requoting their party line. People in schools tend to be 'apolitical' in action, but it's their duty to speak out for future generations. If we are to move the system forward, politicians need to wake up to the scale of the issues raised in this book. We are not talking about this year, this cohort of young people or this parliamentary term. We need urgent, large-scale, long-term change. A significant change would be to move the influence in school policy away from the potential whims of individual politicians and construct policy through a decision-making process that can build more widespread support and clarity of purpose.

- Agree a rota of headteachers to visit the local MPs surgery individually so that you monopolise time. An MP meeting one local headteacher after another, all making the same case for change, would soon be talking to the party whips about their experience. And if this were mirrored many times over, it would have an impact.

- Work with headteachers locally to agree a rota to write a column in local newspapers about the frustrations, futility and failings of managing a school and the impact upon students. Keep the column 'forward looking' and positive, and suggest ways parents can make a difference and get involved.

- Arrange a showing of the film 'Most Likely To Succeed' (available from www.mltsfilm.org or from the Innovation Unit in the UK www. innovationunit.org), together with a community discussion afterwards. It's a great film for stimulating discussions about future-focused learning.

- Invite someone who wrote an essay in this book to come and speak at your school.

- Run a workshop for parents on how they would like their child's education to be future-ready (we can advise).

- Write your own essay/blog post on our website (www.educationforward.co.uk)

Teachers:

- Submit an article for the Class Action magazine (www.classactionmag.com), a new magazine written by teachers, for teachers.
- Just think. Think if there's a better way of doing what you are doing (particularly if you've been doing it for quite a while), whether there's good research to back up what you are doing, whether it's actually making a positive difference for the children in your care, and whether it is genuinely enjoyable and inculcating a lifelong love for learning. And be courageous to raise your questions with others.
- Get connected, discuss issues with colleagues outside your school and break down silos. Teachers *can* influence policy. If presented with the opportunity to meet with journalists, union leaders and politicians, share your concerns, but also offer your solutions.

School Governors:

- Invite parents to buy a copy of this book (or read the free on-line version).
- When governance works it can transform the culture of school; not just holding school leaders to account, but involving the entire body of staff, parents and where possible, the students. Good governance requires leaders to be research-rich and future-focused to support schools to move forward. The best way is for governors to become familiar faces who frequently reward and recognise the work of the staff in their school.

Politicians:

- Recognise that there needs to be change; real, fundamental change rather than tinkering with a system that is often the equivalent of semaphore in the technological age.
- Build an alliance with colleagues to voice some 'forward looking' issues within your party. Challenge the party's special advisers to the education team when their policy ideas address short-term power for the party over long-term benefit for children.
- Invite contributors to this book to come and give you and other colleagues briefings, and to debate the issues. We can support you to develop a new narrative, which is both evidence-based and compelling. We can connect you to initiatives that are happening globally, where education is less parochial and more future-focused. Successful working examples can show that there *is* an alternative.

Parents:

- If you are a parent wondering 'what next?', there are many things you can do for the future. Of course, the issues raised in this book are about your own children but they are also about every other child, not just in Britain, but across the globe. Learning is not something that should be a race against others but a right for every child. It might be easy to think, 'My child has only three years left and nothing will change in that time. I agree, but what can I do?' As this book shows, some of the things affecting children now affected the previous generation…

you…and left as it is the same sorts of things will affect future generations – your grandchildren.

- Please go to your school and ask the governors to debate some of the big questions raised in this book.
- Be in touch with other parents nationally and globally via social media or through channels where you work to share thoughts and ideas.
- Ask positive questions of your school, your child, of governors and proprietors. For example, are you certain that the breadth of the curriculum is really in the long-term interests of your child or that it is too focused on short-term and superficial measures of the school's own performance? Or, is the school providing opportunities for children to develop the things you value as an adult, such as strength of relationships and resilience? The world will move inextricably forward and in twenty years won't be recognisable, so how is your child's school contributing to her or his future success?
- Start an online petition. It's now easy to do. Online campaign groups, like 38 degrees will host your petition: www.you.38degrees.org.uk/petition/new).

We're Not Alone

There are many other groups that share similar sentiments and ambitions to those expressed in this book. Indeed, the over-fragmentation of future-focused groups is a frustration for many of us who want to see a broader shift to more progressive education policies. Collectively, however, they provide a rich bank of resources, ways to take action, and events organisation. This list is by no means exhaustive, but it'll get you started:

United Kingdom

More than A Score (www.morethanascore.co.uk)

A coalition of organisations advocating alternatives to high stakes testing in early years, primary schools and beyond.

Rescue Our Schools (www.rescueourschools.co.uk)

A parent-led campaign group against dogma-driven education policy in state schools, with a very active facebook page.

Slow Education (www.sloweducation.co.uk)

Believes in promoting deep learning in the context of a broad curriculum that recognises the talents of all students.

Whole Education (www.wholeeducation.org)

A dynamic partnership of schools and organisations committed to redefining today's educational offering.

Innovation Unit (www.innovationunit.org)

A social enterprise that grows new solutions to complex social challenges, and whose heartland is education.

EOS Alliance

Big Change (www.bigchange.org)

A social movement that's supporting the next generation to thrive in life, not just exams.

Flip The System (www.flipthesystem.uk)

An advocacy group that seeks to improve education from the inside out by increasing teacher agency.

Ashoka Foundation (www.uk.ashoka.org)

Ashoka is building a global community of Change Leaders who are creating learning ecosystems in which every young person is provided with experiences that empower them to live for the greater good (to become change-makers). Essentially, members are committed to aligning, collaborating and deepening their ecosystemic impact.

International:

Big Picture Learning (www.bigpicture.org)

An international network of hundreds of schools 'where students are actively invested in their learning and are challenged to pursue their interests by a supportive community of educators, professionals, and family members'.

Project XQ Super School (www.xqsuperschool.org)

A social movement in the US committed to 'reimagining high school'. Has lots of great resources to help you change.

Coalition of Essential Schools (www.essentialschools.org)

A long-established coalition of schools and organisations in USA, Japan and Australia, united around 10 'common principles'.

Deeper Learning (www.deeperlearning4all.org)

An initiative by the Hewlett Foundation seeking to make learning more authentic, with greater depth, based upon six interrelated core competencies.

EL Education (www.eleducation.org)

A large network of US schools supporting whole-school transformation with the goal of helping 'students achieve more than they think possible'. A rich source of classroom resources.

We have allowed the education of our children to become an inadequate impoverished experience at a time in history when the need has never been greater for the young to be empowered to shape our collective future. A public education system with profound ideals for all its citizens needs fighting for. Those ideals have been eroded. We have to re-express them for modern conditions.

We cannot make a better future if we cannot imagine it.

If not now, when?

Printed in Great Britain
by Amazon